HERB GARDEN DESIGN

Ethne Clarke

Photographs by Clive Nichols
Watercolours by Jean Sturgis

FRANCES LINCOLN

Frances Lincoln Ltd
4 Torriano Mews
Torriano Avenue
London NW5 2RZ
www.franceslincoln.com

British Library Cataloguing-in-Publication Data
A catalogue record for this book is available from
the British Library

ISBN 0 7112 2011 5

Typeset in Monotype Garamond 11 on 13pt

Printed and bound in Italy by
Officine Grafiche de Agostini

First Frances Lincoln edition 1995
First paperback edition 2002

9 8 7 6 5 4 3 2 1

HALF-TITLE PAGE *Sunflower,* Helianthus annuus
FRONTISPIECE *A traditional box-edged knot garden
filled with herbs*

Please note Any information given in this
book on the use of any herb as a remedy is
purely anecdotal and is not to be taken as a
recommendation. Neither the author nor the
publisher can be held responsible for any
adverse reaction to any herb mentioned
herein.

CONTENTS

Foreword

Herbs are wonderfully sensuous plants, their flavours and scents capable of evoking the most pleasant memories. They take me back to childhood, to the Milwaukee garden where my German grandmother grew dill and caraway, sage and thyme, parsley and chives in narrow beds edging the back yard. A whiff of any of these transports me once again into her kitchen. I can taste the sweet-sourness of her home-preserved dilled cucumbers and smell the pungent caraway baking in the rye bread.

These were the plants I grew in my first herb garden but as my skills as cook and gardener improved, my range became more exotic. In addition, I began to realize that herbs, with their delicate flowers and enticing shapes and textures, were not simply useful, but also among the most beautiful plants that we grow, with a role to play in an ornamental garden.

So what is a herb? It is hard – if not impossible – to say precisely. Traditionally, it is a plant which has some culinary, medicinal or domestic use, or is valued for its scent – already quite a wide-ranging definition. The European herbalists of the Middle Ages and the Renaissance included in their lists of herbs plants which we would regard simply as ornamental: hollyhocks, aquilegias, pinks and other 'cottage-garden' flowers.

Unless we wish to create a herb garden that is entirely traditional, our modern definition can be even wider. Recently I was admiring an especially lush stretch of ornamental border with a knowledgeable friend. Each time I singled out a particular plant she would say 'That's an important medicinal herb in Japan', or 'You can use that to relieve insect bites', or 'The roots of that one are delicious.' Every plant seemed to have a practical application – which is not surprising when you remember that each country has its own flora and accompanying herbal heritage. One gardener's decorative love-in-a-mist is another's cure for stomach-ache.

Forays into the herbals of other cultures open up a wide choice. Daylilies and hostas are part of the oriental diet and *materia medica*. Australia has its own range of Bach flower remedies based on the native flora, while a number of Australian trees – including *Melaleuca alternifolia*, the source of tea-tree oil, *Eucalyptus gunnii*, known as cider gum from the fermented drink that can be made with its sap, and *Hymenosporum flavum*, the seductively perfumed native frangipani – are classed as bush herbs.

Plants native to North America, such as Joe Pye weed, trilliums, bergamot and liatris, were used in the traditional medicines of Native Americans and were later assimilated by the European settlers. The lists of herbs grown as commercial crops by the Shaker communities are a revelation.

South American peoples found culinary uses for dahlias – and they were probably the first to smoke tobacco, *Nicotiana tabacum*, now recognized as a far from beneficial herb. If you garden in a warm and humid climate you might find inspiration in the landscapes of the Brazilian designer Roberto Burle Marx, who made much use of Amazonian rainforest plants. We have all heard about the pharmacological potential of this threatened resource.

This global assessment of the herb kingdom provides an intriguingly varied palette with which to paint our garden scene, and an enormous capability for experiment, which is part of the fun of gardening.

So, in this book I have extended the definition of the term 'herb'. A quick glance at the herb table on pages 118-136 will reveal, in addition to the conventional herbs, a number of less familiar names.

By the same token, herb gardens come in all shapes and sizes, from my grandmother's narrow borders to complete gardens where the planting consists entirely of herbs. You will find in these pages both herb gardens and gardens with herbs. In some, herbs form only a small part of the composition, while in others they set the mood, but in all of them herbs are used to extend the possibilites for garden-making.

The gardens in this book range from traditional knot gardens and other historically inspired designs to more individual schemes where familiar herbs are combined with their purely decorative cousins. In this mixed border, herbs such as cotton lavender and catmint mingle prettily with the ornamental Achillea *'Coronation Gold', blue campanulas and fuchsia-pink hardy* Geranium psilostemon.

PLANNING AND PLANTING

❧

Herbs deserve to be considered as plants from which a satisfying garden picture can be painted. By drawing from the broad palette of leaf and flower colour, shape and texture offered by the world's herbal heritage, we can greatly enrich our gardens.

ABOVE Pulmonaria saccharata, *with its curious splattered variegation and muted colour, is a herb of understated beauty.*

LEFT *In a richly satisfying herbal planting, a haze of blue* Nepeta 'Six Hills Giant' *and soothing green southernwood provide a background for the harmonizing purples, mauves and pinks of irises,* Lavandula stoechas subsp. pedunculata, *chives and* Stachys macrantha 'Superba'.

Herbs to Suit the Site

Surprisingly many exotics transplant well to life in cultivation in climates and conditions different from those in which they evolved. It is often helpful to note where a plant originated in order to assess whether we can grow it in our own gardens. Climatic zones, noted in the herb table, give a broad indication of plants' tolerance of winter cold and summer heat, but a description of the plant's natural habitat offers more information about whether plants prefer sun or shade, dry or moist soil, poor or rich ground. Pulmonarias, for example, do best in moist soil in part-shade, and the flag irises and most primulas like damp, almost boggy conditions; woodland plants such as trilliums relish shade and humus-rich soils. Most herbs are indigenous to regions boasting a Mediterranean type of climate – hot, dry summers and warm, wet winters. However, many will thrive in cooler temperatures as long as the growing conditions are suitable. Generally these herbs prefer soils similar to those of their native habitat – that is, light, sharply draining and gravelly. But any reasonable soil will do as long as it has good drainage. If your garden falls short of the optimum requirements, there are steps you can take to improve conditions: choose a sunny, sheltered site, for a start. Improving the soil can also help matters. Heavy soils, which few herbs enjoy, can be opened up by digging in plenty of gravel.

LEFT *Thyme, winter savory and* Nepeta racemosa *'Snowflake' all enjoy dry, sunny conditions.*

RIGHT *In this damp, partly shaded border, easy-going golden hop threads its way through a mixed planting. Hellebores, ferns,* Luzula nivea *and London pride are moisture-loving and do well here.* Smyrnium perfoliatum *and nectaroscordum are not fussy about their situation.* Euphorbia characias, *however, would be happier in a dry position.*

Choosing a Design

History has provided us with plenty of ideas for herb gardens in formal settings, so having space restrictions and rectilinear boundaries (as many of us do) can be a positive asset rather than a limitation. Formal designs look good in the regularly shaped enclosures adjacent to buildings or within compartmented gardens. But the layout you choose need not be geometric: many of the most inspiring gardening writers have sung the praises of cottage-garden confusion and of natural plant forms softening the hard lines of built structures and rigid ground plans. Recent ecological approaches dispense with any apparent formality – and many herbs are well suited to styles that seek to imitate nature.

A herb garden is any ornamental space planted predominantly with herbs. It does not have to be in the kitchen garden, although, for historical reasons, this is the location that we automatically associate with herbs. In medieval times, before the idea of ornamental gardens had been formed, all plants were grown for a purpose. The best-recorded gardens were those of monasteries, where herbs were most often grown in narrow rectangular beds raised above the level of the paths that separated them. During the early Renaissance in Italy, and later elsewhere in Europe, gardens intended for pleasure developed along more aesthetic lines; some of the prettier herbs crept into the pleasure garden where they were enjoyed for their colour or scent – sometimes in formal conceits such as knots – but the more workaday

The principles of ecological planting can be applied in any design where informal planting is acceptable. Here, southernwood, clary and Loddon Pink lavender – all plants tolerant of dry conditions – thrive in a sunny border at the foot of a wall, while moisture-loving Rambler roses and rhubarb are comfortably placed in deeply dug and composted beds.

A hedge of grey-leaved cotton lavender, Santolina chamaecyparissus *'Nana', combines with box to define the structure of this formal knot garden.*

ones remained in the neatly ordered beds which composed the monastic plan. This design practice was followed when, in response to the emerging science of medicine, the first botanic gardens, dedicated to growing physic herbs, were established at Pisa and Padua in the sixteenth century. A formal scheme of uniform beds made it easier to study the plants.

Regularity and uniformity fell out of fashion in eighteenth-century England, when the park-making activities of Kent, Brown and Repton banned formality in the pleasure grounds surrounding stylish houses. Herbs found refuge in kitchen gardens and physic gardens, and in the garden plots of smallholding farmers and yeomen. It was these gardens that fuelled the Victorian passion for 'cottage gardens', a theme that still preoccupies nostalgically minded designers today. Much contemporary herb garden design is still rooted in the Victorian version of sixteenth- and seventeenth-century gardens, neatly edged with clipped box and never straying far from the parsley-sage-rosemary-and-thyme formula.

Our garden thinking has also been shaped by writers like Eleanour Sinclair Rohde, Frances Bardeswell, Hilda Leyel, Gertrude Jekyll and Vita Sackville-West, and their celebrations of those distant 'golden afternoon' gardens, where plants of all kinds were 'jumbled up together, the tall sheltering the low, and the fragrant justifying their presence even when their colour and form may not; a veritable patchwork of colour . . . Always there is a little pathway of stone or bricks, always there is lavender, and herbs and rosemary and climbing roses whenever support can be found for them.' Thus wrote Edna Walling, Australia's pre-eminent garden designer. The cottage-garden style still influences many of today's small gardens.

More recently an ecological philosophy of planting has evolved, with the emphasis on sustainability achieved through natural balance. This is not a new idea, however. As early as 1870, William Robinson's *The Wild Garden* advocated the planting of hardy 'exotics' in conditions that suit them, 'where they will thrive without further care'. This 'natural' style of planting is ideally suited to herb-growing. In such schemes the herbs and their companions are grouped according to their mutual compatibility determined by requirements of habitat. For example, a large number of herbs prefer dry conditions, are well able to regenerate themselves by self-seeding or layering, and – if planted in compatible groups – will support rather than compete with each other. Anyone living in an area where drought is a problem would do well to investigate the possibilities offered by planting drought-resistant herbs. Conversely, a damp patch of ground would suit a whole range of moisture-loving herbs and their allies – among them sweet flag, flag irises, primulas, meadowsweet, *Lobelia cardinalis*, creeping Jenny and the mint family. In either case, the plants are grouped and intermixed much as they would be in nature.

Garden Structure

When planning a herb garden, you can begin by laying it out carefully with a ruler on paper, or you can charge out into the garden site with bamboo canes and lengths of string. One of the great garden controversies of the past hundred years has been between the advocates of an architectural style of garden design, largely inspired by the formal gardens of the sixteenth and seventeenth centuries, and those who wished to create a naturalistic garden where plants were given the lead and garden style followed their informal habits of growth.

At the turn of the century, battle lines were drawn between Robinson, leading the natural or wild school of thought (bamboo canes and bits of string) and Reginald Blomfield, a leading architect and authority on Renaissance architecture (much inclined to ruler and paper). Respectively, they wrote: 'Nature abhors lines; she is for geometers a reluctant pupil'; and 'The long yew-hedge is clipped and shorn because we want its firm boundary lines . . . The formal garden lends itself readily to designs of smaller gardens within the garden.'

By and large, when applied to the discipline of designing a herb garden, the geometers seem to have taken the day. The foundation of most herb gardens is still box-edged beds punctuated with clipped topiary shapes for emphasis and focus, and with the herb plants arranged by height, with the low-growers to the edges and the tall plants holding the centre or backfield. This kind of garden can be created on any scale. It is particularly good for a herb garden sited close to the house, when it becomes part of the architecture.

Hedges and edgings are the main components which give the formal garden its foundation: vistas are outlined, borders and beds contained, parterres scrolled on to the ground, arbours screened, paths defined. Besides the indispensable box (*Buxus sempervirens* for tall hedges, *B.s.* 'Suffruticosa' for low edging, cultivars of *B. microphylla* in harsher climates), wall germander (*Teucrium × lucidrys*), hyssop, santolina and dwarf varieties of lavender – shrubby herbs that are amenable to clipping – are most often grown for formal outlining. Other relatively neat and compact plants, such as common thyme, chives, thrift – an edging that is especially useful in warm zones – alpine strawberries, the little daisy *Bellis perennis* 'Dresden China', London pride and moss-curled parsley all make satisfactory edgings and would be excellent choices to introduce a touch of formality to a cottage-style garden.

Strong vertical accents help to carry the eye along a vista, to make eye-catchers at the end of a view and to punctuate the formal rhythm of a pattern. Cones and obelisks of clipped box, hornbeam, yew or bay are especially useful for this aesthetic purpose, as are some of the more fanciful topiary shapes, like 'lollipop' standards using honeysuckle, Portugal laurel or similar glossy-leaved evergreens. On a grand scale, a formal grass walk or *allée* may be sheltered by cue-straight rows of pleached lime (linden) trees. Within a planting scheme, perennial or annual climbers such as golden hop, morning glory or jasmine can be trained up frames or poles.

Whereas a formal herb garden can be small-scale, informal gardens require space to breathe. Gentle curves need room to develop if they are to appear graceful rather than pinched; borders need depth in which plant shapes can be played off against one another. There needs to be a sense of landscape beyond to help the truly informal garden seem as though it is merely a corner of paradise captured by the gardener.

The criteria for planning an informal garden are entirely different from those for a formal garden. There may be no clearly defined lines to infill, yet a successful planting needs some sense of composition. Beth Chatto puts it succinctly: '. . . too rigid planning can be static. But having no principles produces chaos in the garden, as elsewhere.' The foundation of the design must depend entirely upon how plants are grouped together and the visually pleasing shapes that this creates within the border.

Start from the ecological/habitat approach, choosing herbal plants that will enjoy your conditions. Assemble the shapes, beginning with the larger woody evergreen and deciduous shrubs chosen for form. These will be the dominant plants within the composition. Then move to sizeable groups of perennials which will establish a theme of leaf and flower colour, positioning them so that late bloomers conceal the earlier plants as they fade. Finally, early spring bulbs and low creeping carpeters can be tucked in around the edges, blurring even further such lines as exist.

Paths are part of the skeleton of a herb garden, whether formal or informal, and in either case must not be mean: main walkways through a garden should be wide enough for two people to walk abreast in comfort – that is, at least 1.5m/5ft wide – while subsidiary paths should be a minimum of 60cm/2ft wide. Paving slabs can be expensive but look marvellous in a formal setting; brick (especially if it is a rich terracotta colour) complements herb plantings particularly well. Gravel from local sources blends in with the surrounding landscape. Wooden slabs have a good rustic look suitable for informal settings, but are treacherously slippery when wet. Grass is inexpensive but high-maintenance, and thyme and camomile are difficult to sustain and should be used only where there is little wear.

A glorious mixture of yellow-leaved herbs is given focus by the skilful placing of a statue.

LEFT *Retaining walls made from local stone and paths of the local gravel ensure that the hard landscaping blends harmoniously into the garden setting.*

ABOVE Saxifraga *'Clarence Elliott'* (top left), *a dwarf relative of London pride, makes a low evergreen edging that bursts into bright colour each spring.* Armeria maritima *'Alba', the white sea thrift (top right), is another useful evergreen edging with the bonus of spring flowers. Moss-curled parsley (bottom left) can be sown as a temporary edging in a herb garden or potager. However, the most popular edging by far is box – common box,* Buxus sempervirens, *dwarf box,* B.s. *'Suffruticosa' (bottom right), or, in a harsh climate, one of the cultivars of* B. microphylla.

Herbs and their Habits

Shrubby herbs contribute a steady presence to any design, requiring only occasional pruning or clipping to keep them in shape. Ground-cover plants and taller accents like climbers and standards also have their permanent place in a scheme and just need seasonal tidy-ups. Annuals and biennials can be more demanding, not just because they have to be sown in the first place (or weeded from the 'wrong' places, as many freely self-seed), but also because in a season they can zoom from bare earth anywhere up to eye-level or even beyond (angelica provides a prime example), transforming the look of the garden. Tall herbaceous perennials can also be demanding. Most tall-growers have rigid stems, so staking is not always necessary (or desirable), but cutting out faded flowers and stems will help to keep plants looking fresh.

So, among the factors to consider, when planning what herbs to place where, are not only the potential height and spread of the mature plant, but also whether the plant is perennial, annual or whatever. You will need to know whether to count it as a permanent resident of the garden or a transient feature that will have to be resown or replanted. Get to know the habit of growth of each plant so that you can predict how its performance in the garden will change over the seasons and from year to year. Visit as many gardens as you can to assess the real-life impact of different plants.

The herb table (pages 118-136) will tell you which herbs are annuals or biennials, completing their growth cycle in one or two years; herbaceous perennials that regrow over several years from an underground rootstock; or woody-stemmed perennials or sub-shrubs that survive for many years. There are also some bulbs, and a few trees and climbers.

The fact that so many herbs are of Mediterranean origin can make it difficult to sustain the interest of the herb garden through the year. Herbaceous perennials from the Mediterranean come into growth in autumn or early spring and need to complete the leaf/flower/seed cycle and retreat below ground before the desiccating summer heat of their native habitat would make it impossible to sustain vegetative growth above ground. With all these plants hurrying to grow to maturity while conditions are favourable, is it surprising that our herb gardens can look a wasteland by midsummer?

However, the shrubby plants, especially the evergreens – with green or grey leaves – provide a permanent framework that keeps the herb garden in shape. Again, plants such as trilliums, hostas, male ferns, fumitory and aconites, from cool temperate climates (north America, northern Europe and the Far East) can make a contribution to a garden's appearance throughout the year. Annual herbs of Mediterranean origin can also help. In their native habitat they germinate in autumn and overwinter in seed-leaf stage, bursting into rapid growth in spring to flower, set seed and die before summer. However, in cooler climates with higher rainfall, germination can take place in spring as well as autumn, and successional sowing makes plants available to fill gaps. Finally some perennials, cut to the ground and fed generously in early summer, can provide another show.

Annuals and biennials, such as these foxgloves (left), can be allowed to seed themselves around the garden for a random effect. The carefully orchestrated stretch of border (right) is composed almost entirely of perennials and shrubs.

Shaping the Planting

Once you have decided what style of garden you wish to create and have some idea of the type of herbs you would like to use, the next stage is to organize the composition, using the herbs' shape and form to best advantage. All herbs, from tiny thymes to towering angelica, have form, which is their habit of growth: low and bun-shaped, pencil-thin and upright, loose and branching, neat and compact.

The way shape is deployed to fill in the structure of the garden plan depends upon the effect you hope to create. Formality requires a repetition of uniform shapes: clipped cones of box, bay trees or lemon verbena trained as standards, fastigiate yews, clipped edgings of box, teucrium and hyssop are all staples of formal herb gardens. Less formally, the repeated use of the same plant in a scheme also creates a rhythm, as does the repeated use of mound-forming shrub roses or herbs such as sage, or low-edgers like thyme, pinks or clumps of alpine strawberries. Most often these shapes are constructed around a main axis or central point to make a more or less symmetrically balanced design. But even within an informal cottage-garden design or an ecological planting scheme, repetition of shape – and not necessarily of the same plant – should be a consideration. Repeated groups of evergreen (or ever-grey) herbs can be used to anchor and unify the planting.

The impact of a plant is very much influenced by the shape and texture of its leaves. The leaves of most plants appear long before the blossoms and linger after the petals fall. This is especially true of herbs, where the fleeting flowers are often of the most subtle tints, and the foliage can steal the show. It may be bold and brassy, like that of the pure yellow lemon balm 'All Gold'; soft and ferny, like bronze fennel; grey and spiky, like curry plant; or rich burgundy-red, like orach. It can be

ABOVE *In a planting that is harmonious in colour but varied in shape and texture, alliums are set against bold angelica leaves, the winged flowers of* Lavandula stoechas *subsp.* pedunculata, *sword-like irises and palmate alchemilla leaves. The leaves of purple sage pick up the colour of the flowers.*

FAR LEFT *Red orach seedlings sprout among rows of oakleaf lettuce and flat-leaved parsley.*

LEFT *The handsome spires of foxgloves appear through a mist of filigree fennel leaves.*

broad or needle-like, smooth and shiny, rough and hairy, felted, matt or semi-gloss.

All these qualities of shape, colour and texture can be played off against each other, exploited for their contrasts or blended harmoniously to create absorbing garden pictures. For example, if you hold a sage leaf and a bay leaf side by side, you will notice that the dull surface of the sage leaf absorbs the light, while the glossy bay leaf reflects it. This demonstrates the way subjects that absorb light visually recede, while those that reflect it appear

to advance. You can use this to advantage in your overall design: to blur the edges of a planting, use dull-leaved plants like sage or catmint; for emphasis, choose a shiny-textured subject such as bay, holly or box.

Texture also affects the collective appearance of plants: from a distance a group of broad-leaved plants has a uniformity that makes a more solid impact than the effect created by a mass of small-leaved plants, whose 'spotty', indistinct outlines have a hazy, insubstantial quality.

Colour in the Herb Garden

Herbs suffer the great injustice of being considered rather boring when it comes to flower colour. There are exceptions, of course. In fact, there are some real stunners among the herbs – no one could accuse a sunflower or a marigold of being low-key, and some of the richest reds and purples are found among the old roses, bergamots and salvias. None the less, it must be acknowledged that herb flowers in general tend to be small and understated. To avoid a spotty effect, plant them in bold masses – ribbons of lavender, swathes of catmint, a stand of *Nicotiana sylvestris*. There is also strength in numbers when a subtle tint is picked up and reinforced by its neighbours. Many herb flowers come in wishy-washy pinky-mauve tints that are inconspicuous in themselves but can be used to underpin or blend together stronger pinks, lilacs, lavenders and violet-blues, joining forces to create a harmonious whole.

Attitudes to colour are intensely subjective: you must plan according to your own colour preferences. For instance, I can never quite see the charm of the all-white gardens which so many people find enchanting, although I do admit that seen by moonlight they have an ethereal beauty. Other monochrome schemes appeal to me more. A much-loved corner of my garden is planted with restful blues: the lavender-blue catmint 'Six Hills Giant', deep purple Hidcote lavender and blue hyssop, with spikes of purplish-blue *Verbena bonariensis* waving about above it all. Schemes based on sunshine-yellow flowers amid golden foliage can also work very well.

More lively than any monochrome scheme are those in which different hues are combined. Following the most basic colour theory, and the one that seems to me the most workable in designing a planting, I would advocate the use of the complementary colours that are opposite

to each other on the colour wheel (blue and orange, purple and yellow, red and green); or triads of adjacent colours (red, orange, yellow; yellow, green, blue; violet, red, orange).

In her *Colour Schemes for the Flower Garden*, Gertrude Jekyll described the effects to be achieved with complementary colours in a long border. She also expressed a desire to create a whole series of gardens of restricted colouring, but admonished colourists not to spoil the effect for the sake of a word; a blue garden may be made to look even bluer by just the slightest touch of the right tint of its yellow complement.

The effects of colour interactions can be used in the garden to modify colours, to give a scheme depth and highlights and to create particular moods. Take the blue scheme

described earlier. If I were to scatter some yellow through it, perhaps *Achillea* 'Moonshine', or a low-growing golden rod like *Solidago* 'Crown of Rays', or *Hemerocallis* 'Stella de Oro' (or all three), the effect would be quite different. The tensions set up by the colour contrasts would be as buzzy as the bees in the catmint, and a scene of understated tranquillity would be transformed into one of lively activity.

Colour can also be used to enhance the scale of the garden and to emphasize or play down various aspects. It is generally experienced that warm colours – reds, oranges, yellows – advance visually, while those at the cool end of the spectrum – blues, greens, violets – recede. So if you want to make a narrow space seem wider, plant blues, greys and mauves along the sides; save the hot colours for bold visual statements that draw the eye towards them.

Above all, don't be afraid of using colour – and don't be intimidated by thoughts of good taste. The eminent landscape architect Sir Geoffrey Jellicoe wrote that 'The private garden remains constant as the peculiar expression of the individual', and by peculiar he meant unique, not odd. Remember that you are making your herb garden for your pleasure, and then the way in which you choose to combine the elements of its design will be your peculiar expression.

Every season has its own characteristic colour, beginning with the pale watery tints of early spring, seen (above left) in the spidery lemon-tinged flowers of witch hazel. The year continues through the blues and mauves of early summer to the bright yellows and oranges of high summer, when pot marigolds, nasturtiums, Bupleurum falcatum *and love-in-a-mist seedheads scramble beneath a gauze of* Hordeum jubatum, *the squirrel-tail grass (right).*

ABOVE *In this subtle planting, the glaucous foliage of* dianthus *and* Allium karataviense *brings out the blue in the leaves of the variegated sage, while the* white and raspberry-pink in the sage are echoed by the white dianthus flowers and the dusky pink allium seedheads.

OPPOSITE, ABOVE *Rich purple Hidcote lavender with crimson* Lychnis coronaria.

OPPOSITE, BELOW *Lavender violas with catmint.*

Scent and Sound for Sensuality

Two invisible but important dimensions that contribute to the enjoyment of the herb garden are scent and sound. The pleasure derived from the catmint corner in my garden is greatly enhanced by the hum of the bumblebees foraging among the flowers. The rustle of bamboo as a breeze stirs through the canes is as soothing as the murmur of flowing water. However, scent is probably more apparent to our senses when enjoying a garden.

Few of the herbal plants release their perfume on the breeze; it can be savoured only when the foliage, stems or petals are crushed, brushed against or otherwise bruised, or when the sun's warmth causes the oil glands in the leaves to secrete their fragile aromas. For this reason, you should position the finest of the scented herbs in the garden where their perfumes can be easily appreciated.

The incense rose, *Rosa primula*, grows near my kitchen door. It is a hardy, sturdy rose, covered in tiny butter-yellow flowers from spring to early summer, and makes a bush up to 2m/7ft tall. On humid summer evenings, or in the morning as the mist is just burning off, an exquisite breath of frankincense and myrrh is offered each time I come and go from the garden.

Across the yard there is a hedge of sweetbriar roses and old English lavender. In the warmth, the smell of green apples given off by the rose foliage, combined with the spicy lavender, is heavenly. The chore of mowing the strip of grass at the foot of the hedge is a pleasure, for the mingled fragrances are released each time I sweep by.

As soon as it is warm enough, I put pot-grown orange and lemon trees on the terrace, in company with a collection of scented pelargoniums. Their fragrance, combined with that of a wall-trained fig tree, is like distilled essence of Tuscany.

OPPOSITE *A field of lavender in full flower perfumes the air for miles around, while a single bush will bring welcome scent to the smallest garden.*

ABOVE *Some roses perfume the garden with abandon, but the Hybrid Musk 'Penelope' has a gentle scent, at its most poignant on a still midsummer evening.*

Herbs for Honeybees

In addition to our own pleasure, there is another reason to concentrate on scent and colour when planting a herb garden; and that is to attract honeybees. Bees are so beneficial to us, pollinating flowers, making honey and animating the garden with their industry and the soothing lilt of their buzz, that planting according to their needs is the least we can do.

It is primarily colour and pattern which attract honeybees to flowers, but scent does play a role. Scout bees identify an especially abundant patch of pollen- or nectar-rich flowers, and return to the hive taking the flower perfume to the workers, who use it to recognize the correct area to forage.

The fuzzy orange and black bumblebees begin their forays in spring, visiting early-flowering bulbs, crocus in particular. These can be scattered beneath later-flowering ground-covers like aubrieta and lamiums. Forget-me-nots, primroses, cowslips, violets, cotoneaster, the flowers of strawberries and blackberries, pears, plums and apples, can all be used to give early forage, and flower colour, to a bee garden. The main plantings, however, must be devoted to summer, the season when the shiny little honeybees are at their busiest. Catmint, lavender, hyssop, winter savory, sage, rosemary and thyme are among the herbal plants most loved by honeybees.

They also like peace and quiet, so a garden that is to attract bees should be sited where there is shelter and serenity. A hedge is preferable to a wall for protection; there can be terrific downdraughts on the lee-side of a solid windbreak, but the branches and foliage of a hedge break up the air currents. If there are a few apple or plum trees nearby, so much the better. But choose, if you can, a sunny place, because bees prefer to work flowers that are in the sun rather than in the shade. Don't we all?

Herb gardens provide forage for many nectar-feeding birds and insects. Honeybees are among the most valued guests, and planting specifically for their needs has benefits for gardeners as well as insects. Bergamot (below left), thyme (below right) and catmint (opposite) are prime bee flowers.

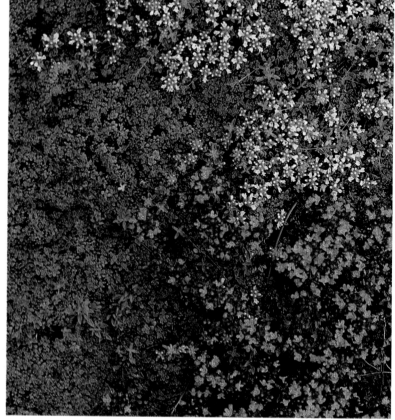

DESIGNS FOR HERB GARDENS

❧

Herbs may be grown in a garden or a section of a garden reserved solely for them, or they can play a supporting role as part of the larger landscape picture. In the widely varied gardens shown in this book, familiar plants and their exotic cousins have been gathered together from the world's herbal heritage. Modern herb gardeners can follow this tradition to make the most of soil and site to provide ideal growing conditions, or simply to invoke the gentle spirit of past gardens and their creators.

ABOVE *In a planting that makes the most of variations of shape, texture and colour, feathery soft green mounds of southernwood are carefully positioned between the silvery, felted leaves of lamb's ears and the narrower leaves of* Artemisia ludoviciana.

LEFT *A profuse planting of free-growing herbs is contained within the formal structure of a clipped box hedge.*

Flower and Herb Knots

Knot gardens recall the time of the Tudors, when pattern books popularized a wealth of varied designs. One of the earliest known references comes from a schoolboys' Latin grammar of 1519:

> The knot garden serveth for pleasure;
> the potte garden for profitte.
> *Horti serviunt voluptati: Horti holitorius utilitati.*

Among the most renowned knot gardens of the period was the one made by Cardinal Wolsey at

The shapes of two of the flowery knots form 'A' and 'T', the owners' initials, while another two are based on the family emblem of a cross within a square. The herb-filled beds beyond are laid out in a simpler geometric pattern.

Hampton Court Palace. It was sited below the windows of the Cardinal's private rooms, so that he could gaze down on the elaborate geometric and fanciful emblems delineated in clipped box and herbs of all kinds.

Knots can be adapted to almost any setting: their tidy design means that they are as well suited to a small plot as to a position in extensive grounds. They can be based on abstract designs or on motifs that have some significance to the gardener. The knot gardens shown on these pages form part of the gardens of a sixteenth-century moated manor house, although the knots themselves were created only in the 1980s. The two knot gardens are spread out below the grass rampart that borders the moat. Each is composed of four squares: one set is filled with flowers that were commonly planted in gardens

before 1750, and the other is devoted to herbs – one garden for pleasure, the other for profit.

The designs here are what is known as 'closed' knots, one of two styles current in the sixteenth century. An open knot was one in which the lines of hedging did not intersect, so it was possible to stroll around within the pattern gathering little tussie-mussie nosegays of herbs and flowers. If the hedges interlaced, the knot was closed and you could only drift around the perimeter to do the gathering and sniff the sweet perfumes. One of the most popular closed-knot patterns of the sixteenth and seventeenth centuries resembles the links of a chain crossed and interwoven with a circle, and is known as the 'True Lover's Knot'. In one pattern book this design was captioned 'Here

1m 1m
3ft 3ft

→

The triangular beds of the herb knots are planted with a variety of culinary and medicinal herbs, while beyond lie beds of old shrub roses, edged with catmint, lavender or hyssop. High yew hedges enclose the garden.

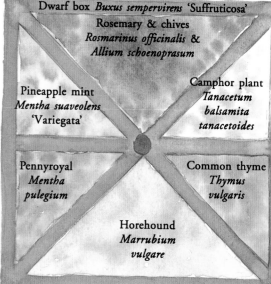

Dwarf box *Buxus sempervirens* 'Suffruticosa'

Rosemary & chives
Rosmarinus officinalis &
Allium schoenoprasum

Pineapple mint
Mentha suaveolens
'Variegata'

Camphor plant
*Tanacetum
balsamita
tanacetoides*

Pennyroyal
*Mentha
pulegium*

Common thyme
*Thymus
vulgaris*

Horehound
*Marrubium
vulgare*

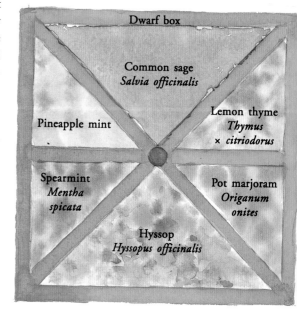

Dwarf box

Common sage
Salvia officinalis

Pineapple mint

Lemon thyme
*Thymus
× citriodorus*

Spearmint
*Mentha
spicata*

Pot marjoram
*Origanum
onites*

Hyssop
Hyssopus officinalis

I have made the true lover's knot. To tie it in marriage was never my lot.' The knot motifs here tell a happier tale. One pair of the flower-filled beds takes as inspiration the cross within a square which forms the family fret. The other two beds incorporate the letters 'A' and 'T', the first-name initials of the owners.

The herb knots, in keeping with their contents, are much simpler: crossing lines of box divide the squares into triangular beds, each devoted to a single herb, or two at most. Standard clipped box balls mark the centre of each square, like thumb tacks pinning the design to a drawing board.

Box has long been the favourite shrub for creating the pattern of knot gardens, but before its advent thyme, hyssop and lavender were popular. These were among the herbs recommended in 1616 by the writer Gervase Markham, who also mentioned camomile and pennyroyal. (It is hard to imagine pennyroyal as an edging herb – it would be rather low and snaky.) In the gardens of Renaissance Italy, clumps of the small lawn daisy, *Bellis perennis*, were used, as were wild strawberries.

A great virtue of clipped box is its neatness and uniformity. In this design all the knot hedges are of dwarf box and all are of roughly the same height. However, by planting some of the lines with variegated or golden box and clipping the hedges so that they appear to go over and under each other when they intersect, a more varied appearance can be achieved. Because it is evergreen, a box knot is interesting throughout the year, continuing to contribute to the garden scene when flowers and herbs have retreated below ground. A varied and undulating knot pattern can be that much more intriguing, particularly in the winter garden.

To many people, the great charm of a flower-filled knot is seeing the sprays of flowers waving about above the box pattern like many-coloured pennants. Here the celebration

The success of a knot garden hinges on meticulous maintenance. Hedges must be kept neatly trimmed, edges should be knife-edge sharp. In this garden a brick edging reinforces the perfectly maintained lines of the knot patterns.

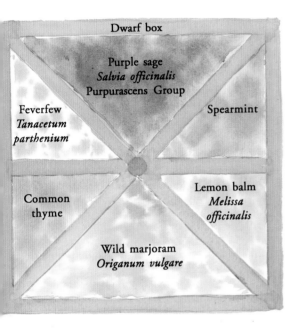

Dwarf box

Purple sage
Salvia officinalis
Purpurascens Group

Feverfew
Tanacetum parthenium

Spearmint

Common thyme

Lemon balm
Melissa officinalis

Wild marjoram
Origanum vulgare

Dwarf box

Russian sage & pot marigolds
*Perovskia atriplicifolia &
Calendula officinalis*

Thymus vulgaris
'Silver Posie'

Chives
Allium schoenoprasum

Good King Henry
Chenopodium bonus-henricus

Bowle's mint
Mentha × villosa alopecuroides

Winter savory
Satureja montana

begins in early spring with grape hyacinths, species crocus in variety, lily-of-the-valley and *Tulipa clusiana*, which is commonly known as the Lady tulip and is of great antiquity in gardens. The spotted leaves and pink flowers of lungwort supplement the emerging foliage of herbaceous perennials such as dictamnus, monarda, Madonna and regal lilies. These are the real banner flowers. Ever-present grey tussocks of Cheddar pinks and *Santolina chamaecyparissus* make pools of brightness in the shady quarters.

All this clear bright flower colour is in marked contrast to the more subtle tints of leaf and flower in the herb knots. Few of these plants send volunteers above the ramparts, making instead mounds of green, grey, purple, silver and gold: marjoram, winter savory, horehound, common and purple sage, and common, lemon and 'Silver Posie' thyme. The one explosion of colour comes from the common pot marigold, *Calendula officinalis*. Its petals have brightened our gardens, flavoured our food and made healing broths ever since the first knots were formed.

Beyond the knot gardens are rectangular rose beds filled with the striped Gallica Rosa Mundi and edged with catmint. Beyond these lies a further rose garden devoted to old shrub roses: one bed of Alba and species roses, another of Centifolia and Moss roses, one of Gallicas, Damasks and Bourbons and one more filled with China, Rugosa and Hybrid Perpetuals. Each bed is edged with lavender 'Hidcote' or hyssop, and the roses are interplanted with hellebores, thyme, lady's mantle, purple violas, lilies, white foxgloves and blue and white *Campanula persicifolia*. The Rosa Mundi beds and the tall yew hedges along the sides of the knots completely enclose the garden, trapping the flower and herb scents and ensuring an atmosphere of timeless tranquillity within a modern herb garden that is firmly rooted in the past.

A Thyme Garden

This small box-edged bed, like an emerald jewel box, contains a collection of thymes. The plan could be expanded to include a far wider selection of the many varieties of thyme in cultivation.

Thyme requires a well-drained soil and plenty of sun to do well. If it is overshadowed by bolder neighbours, the leaves drop, its habit becomes straggly and eventually the plant fades away. For this reason it is best grown in isolation, creeping along the cracks in a paved path, forming mats in gravel gardens, planted in drystone walls – or, as shown here, in a bed devoted to thyme.

It is hard to improve upon Vita Sackville-West's description of the thyme lawns she planted at Sissinghurst; it appears under the date for 18 June 1950 in the collection of her writings, *In Your Garden*. She explains how she tried without success to plant two forsaken windswept beds and then hit upon the idea of planting them up entirely with cultivated or garden forms of wild thyme (*Thymus serpyllum*). The ground-hugging thymes were not damaged by wind and when they were in flower the beds were alive with honeybees, thyme being one of their favourite plants. The thyme beds looked 'like a Persian carpet laid out of doors'.

The specific name *serpyllum* derives from the Latin *serpere*, 'to creep', and from this group come many of the best carpeters. With flowers in shades of pink, rosy red and white, some cultivars are variegated while others have dark green glossy foliage or bright apple-green leaves.

Although there is quite enough variety within the *serpyllum* species, there are others I would not want to be without, particularly *T. pseudolanuginosus*, which quickly spreads to cover the ground with a fuzz of blue-green woolly foliage. Some of the varieties and cultivars of

In this box-edged bed different varieties of thyme merge together to make a simple herb carpet.

common thyme, *T. vulgaris*, make further colour contributions: *T. v. aureus* offering a touch of bright yellow and 'Silver Posie' creamy white. Then there is the dimension of scent. Consider the lemony-scented *T. × citriodorus* 'Bertram Anderson, or *T. herba-barona*, for its caraway-scented leaves. Any of these would also add vertical interest should you find the idea of a totally flat garden too monotonous.

If the thyme plants are happy, as they will be if the soil is well-drained, they will rapidly knit together to make a solid colourful mat. Thyme is a greedy feeder, so a regular dose of general-purpose fertilizer will help the plants keep their vigour. Other than that, all they need is to be clipped after flowering. In a small area this can easily be done with hand shears, but if the thyme garden is too large for this, use a strimmer. It takes a little practice to keep the cutting thread low enough to remove the flowers but not so low that it digs into the plants themselves. Obviously, if common thymes are included extra care has to be taken to avoid lopping the plants off at the base.

Thymus herba-barona

Thymus serpyllum *'Pink Chintz'*

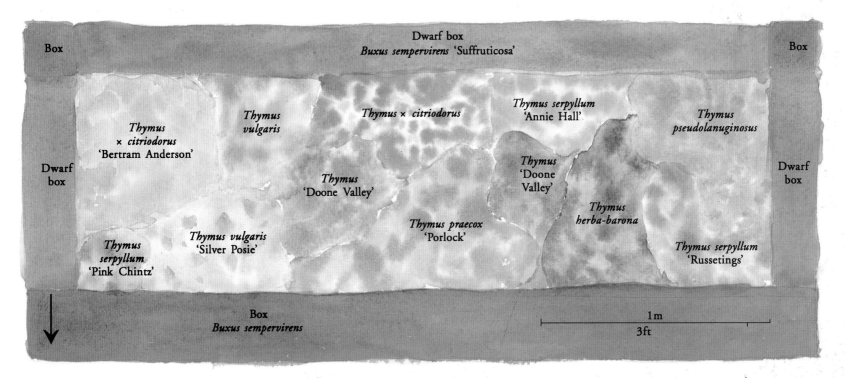

Box

Dwarf box
Buxus sempervirens 'Suffruticosa'

Box

Dwarf box

Thymus × citriodorus 'Bertram Anderson'

Thymus vulgaris

Thymus × citriodorus

Thymus serpyllum 'Annie Hall'

Thymus pseudolanuginosus

Thymus 'Doone Valley'

Thymus 'Doone Valley'

Thymus serpyllum 'Pink Chintz'

Thymus vulgaris 'Silver Posie'

Thymus praecox 'Porlock'

Thymus herba-barona

Thymus serpyllum 'Russetings'

Dwarf box

Box
Buxus sempervirens

1m

3ft

A Formal Herb Garden

A number of the gardens featured in this book are mixed, in the sense that they combine functional herbs with their decorative relatives and with other herbaceous plants that have no known herbal use. The garden shown here, however, is entirely composed of conventional herbs, and it illustrates how a knowledge of herbs and their uses can be allied to a strong visual perception to create a garden that satisfies all the senses.

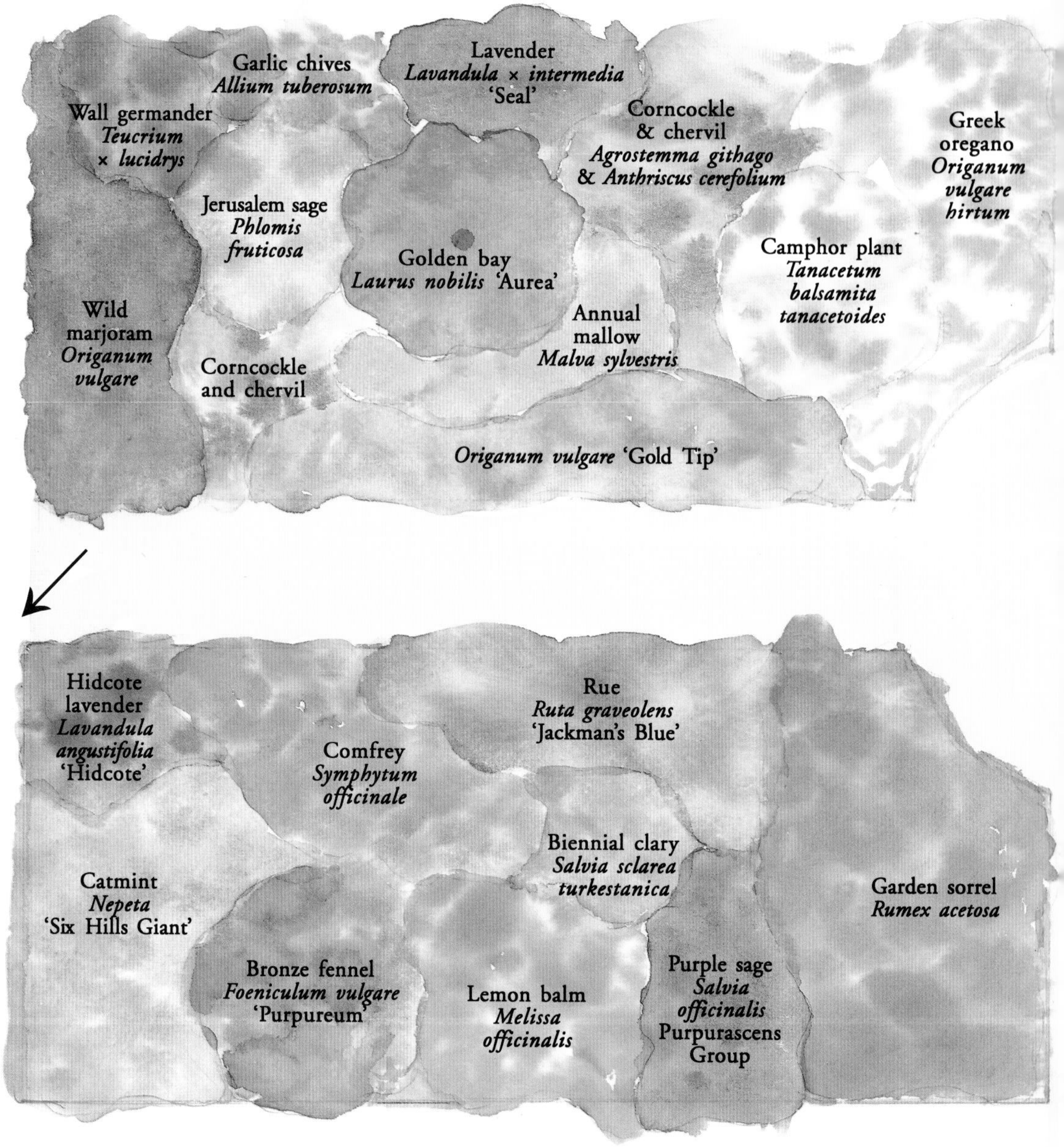

The setting is a country house hotel in north-west Norfolk. The climate in this part of England is especially agreeable, with low rainfall and more hours of sunshine than in most of Britain. The soil is fertile and the proximity to the sea lessens the threat of frost damage. The conditions are just what is needed to grow shrubby herbs of Mediterranean origins in formal beds, with little risk of the sudden blanks in the planting that are so often caused by a combination of cold and damp.

The brick walls around three sides of the garden help too, storing up the sun's heat during the day and throwing it out on to the garden at night. The remaining side is screened by a rose-covered rustic trellis which acts as a windbreak. The saying is that a Norfolk wind is lazy: it goes right through you rather than around. There are many other places regularly afflicted by a stiff breeze – including Chicago, my home town. Gardening when you and the plants are being blown horizontal is no fun, but it is amazing what shelter a simple structure like a screen of wooden poles can offer. Screens also cut down on the turbulence often encountered around walls and buildings.

Familiar diagonal or square grid trellis, woven hurdles – anything a climbing plant can be tethered to – will improve the situation. One of the simplest windbreaks I have seen is made from inexpensive wooden laths 3cm/1¼in wide, arranged horizontally about 2.5cm/1in apart and nailed to posts. Left to weather naturally or stained a dark forest-green, it will snake its way through a garden (the lath is quite pliable, so curves are possible), giving protection where it is most needed.

The garden here follows the traditional plan of a long central axis with crossing paths dividing the space into planting beds. In all there are eight beds, planted with herbs cultivated for their medicinal, culinary or domestic uses. The plan shows about half of the garden: most of the herbs from this area are destined to be made

Garlic chives
Allium tuberosum

Lavender
Lavandula × intermedia
'Seal'

Wall germander
Teucrium × lucidrys

Corncockle & chervil
Agrostemma githago & Anthriscus cerefolium

Greek oregano
Origanum vulgare hirtum

Jerusalem sage
Phlomis fruticosa

Golden bay
Laurus nobilis 'Aurea'

Camphor plant
Tanacetum balsamita tanacetoides

Wild marjoram
Origanum vulgare

Annual mallow
Malva sylvestris

Corncockle and chervil

Origanum vulgare 'Gold Tip'

Hidcote lavender
Lavandula angustifolia 'Hidcote'

Rue
Ruta graveolens 'Jackman's Blue'

Comfrey
Symphytum officinale

Biennial clary
Salvia sclarea turkestanica

Catmint
Nepeta 'Six Hills Giant'

Garden sorrel
Rumex acetosa

Bronze fennel
Foeniculum vulgare 'Purpureum'

Lemon balm
Melissa officinalis

Purple sage
Salvia officinalis Purpurascens Group

Chives
Allium schoenoprasum

Rosa
'Sandringham
Centenary'

Sweet marjoram
*Origanum
majorana*

Mignonette
Reseda odorata

*Arnica
chamissonis*

Gold-variegated sage
Salvia officinalis
'Icterina'

Annual
mallow

*Helichrysum
splendidum*

*Linum
perenne*

Agastache rugosa

Common
thyme
*Thymus
vulgaris*

Pot marigold
Calendula officinalis

*Veronica
cinerea*

Hyssop
*Hyssopus
officinalis*

Origanum vulgare
'Golden Shine'

Wall germander
*Teucrium
× lucidrys*

1m
3ft

1m
3ft

Garlic chives, Allium tuberosum

Lavender
*Lavandula
angustifolia*
'Princess
Blue'

Gold-variegated
lemon balm
Melissa officinalis
'Aurea'

Common sage
Salvia officinalis

Lavandula angustifolia
'Princess Blue'

Bronze
fennel

Bronze fennel

Goat's rue
Galega officinalis

Sweet
cicely
*Myrrhis
odorata*

Lovage
*Levisticum
officinale*

Rosa
'Sandringham
Centenary'

Sweet cicely

into potpourri, garlands and dried floral arrangements, all used to decorate the guest rooms.

For foundation planting each bed includes shrubby herbs chosen for their foliage and contrasting either in colour or shape: blue-grey feathery rue and purple-leaved sage; golden bay and pale *Phlomis fruticosa*; golden sage with hyssop, thyme and teucrium; broad-leaved common sage with narrow-leaved lavender 'Princess Blue'.

Thought has also been given to the way in which the planting of each bed relates to its

Wild marjoram, Origanum vulgare

neighbour, so that, for example, Greek oregano on one side of the cross-axial path is directly opposite sweet marjoram on the other; and on either side of the main path the blue foliage of rue complements the marjoram 'Gold Tip'.

At first sight the juxtaposition of tall and short plants seems fairly random. In fact, beds that are diagonally opposed correspond by height. Thus in one bed the central golden bay with its companions camphor plant and phlomis relates to its kitty-corner partner and the masses of sweet cicely, lovage, bronze fennel and goat's rue planted there.

Because we tend to clip herb plants back hard – snipping them off regularly either for cooking or through some misguided effort to keep the herb garden tidy – we often miss out on the fragile charm of herb flowers. Lavender, of course, is an exception, as are hyssop and teucrium – unless the latter two are used as hedging; in which case, off with their blue and lavender-pink heads. Since this is essentially an ornamental herb garden the herbs are allowed to grow on to flower, and by late summer the display is colourful enough to satisfy the most romantic garden-lover. The mist of mingled marjoram, thymes, rue, oregano, lemon balm and sage flowers is soporific, particularly on a warm afternoon and in the company of foraging honeybees.

Chives also rarely get a chance to flower. Leave a clump to bloom and fluffy purple pom-pons will be the reward. Use them in salads: they taste just like onion and the mauve colour is a perfect complement to multi-green leaves. In this garden, however, the border-grown chives are gathered when the flowers are at their peak for drying. To be sure the blooms retain their shape, each flower stem is dropped feet first through a small mesh

Within the formal structure of this garden the herbs are not constantly snipped back but are allowed to flower and seed with profusion. A bay tree trained as a standard, and with its branches clipped to make a shaggy mophead, marks the crossing of the paths.

screen so that it is suspended by its head; the stalk dries arrow-straight and the flower-head is kept prettily round. The garlic chive's white flowers are given the same treatment.

The permanent planting is relieved with a spangling of annuals. A scattering of self-sown cherry-pink corncockles that look as if they have strayed in from nearby fields, a handful of annual mallow and dots of vivid orange pot marigolds are all at home in this mellow scene.

ABOVE LEFT *The solid grey-green of* Mentha × rotundifolia *sets off the variegated leaves of pineapple mint,* M. suaveolens 'Variegata'.

ABOVE RIGHT *The bright yellow bosses of the daisy-flowered camphor plant,* Tanacetum balsamita *var.* tanacetoides, *pick up the colour in the yellow-flushed foliage of* Origanum vulgare 'Gold Tip'.

RIGHT *The beds around the foot of the sheltering wall surrounding the herb garden provide a home for tall-growing herbs, including comfrey, bronze fennel,* Foeniculum vulgare 'Purpureum', *and clary,* Salvia sclarea *var.* turkestanica. *Artemisia, toadflax and lavender 'Loddon Pink' line the path.*

A Low-allergen Garden

The sneeze factor in any kind of gardening can be high and while mildly irritating for most of us, for allergy sufferers it can be intolerable, turning the garden into a torture chamber, and making gardening a pastime to be avoided. However, in a herb garden like this one the incidence of events that produce allergic reactions is much reduced.

The dimensions of this garden can, of course, be increased or reduced according to the space available, although thought should be given to the scale of the brick or paving stone used in relation to the size of the plot. The criss-cross paths give comfortable access to all parts of the garden, for both tending and harvesting the plants, and the triangles-within-triangles of herbs ensure not only a pleasing design but also ample space for the herbs to spread themselves.

In this clever design low-growing thymes and oregano are backed by taller sage, tarragon and mint. Variegated lemon balm, potted to lend extra height, makes a dramatic central feature. The lip of the pot has been painted to match the brick of the path, and the colours of the herbs, from golden marjoram to purple sage, are complementary.

Herbs are ideally suited to a low-allergen garden since many are labiates and therefore insect-pollinated rather than wind-pollinated. This eliminates wind-borne pollen, one of the culprits for allergic responses. Also, the scent of herbs is in the foliage rather than in the flowers, another advantage because heavy floral scents can trigger adverse reactions. Few herbs suffer from mildew or fungal diseases, so wind-borne mould spores are unlikely to be present.

Dust is unacceptable so the beds are well covered with foliage to blanket the soil, and the paths are lined with hard brick (large-grade gravel or durable ground-covering plants would also serve the purpose). Grass does not have a place in this garden since mowing can irritate allergic people. Non-allergic people gain, too – one of the side benefits of this low-allergen garden is that it is also low-maintenance.

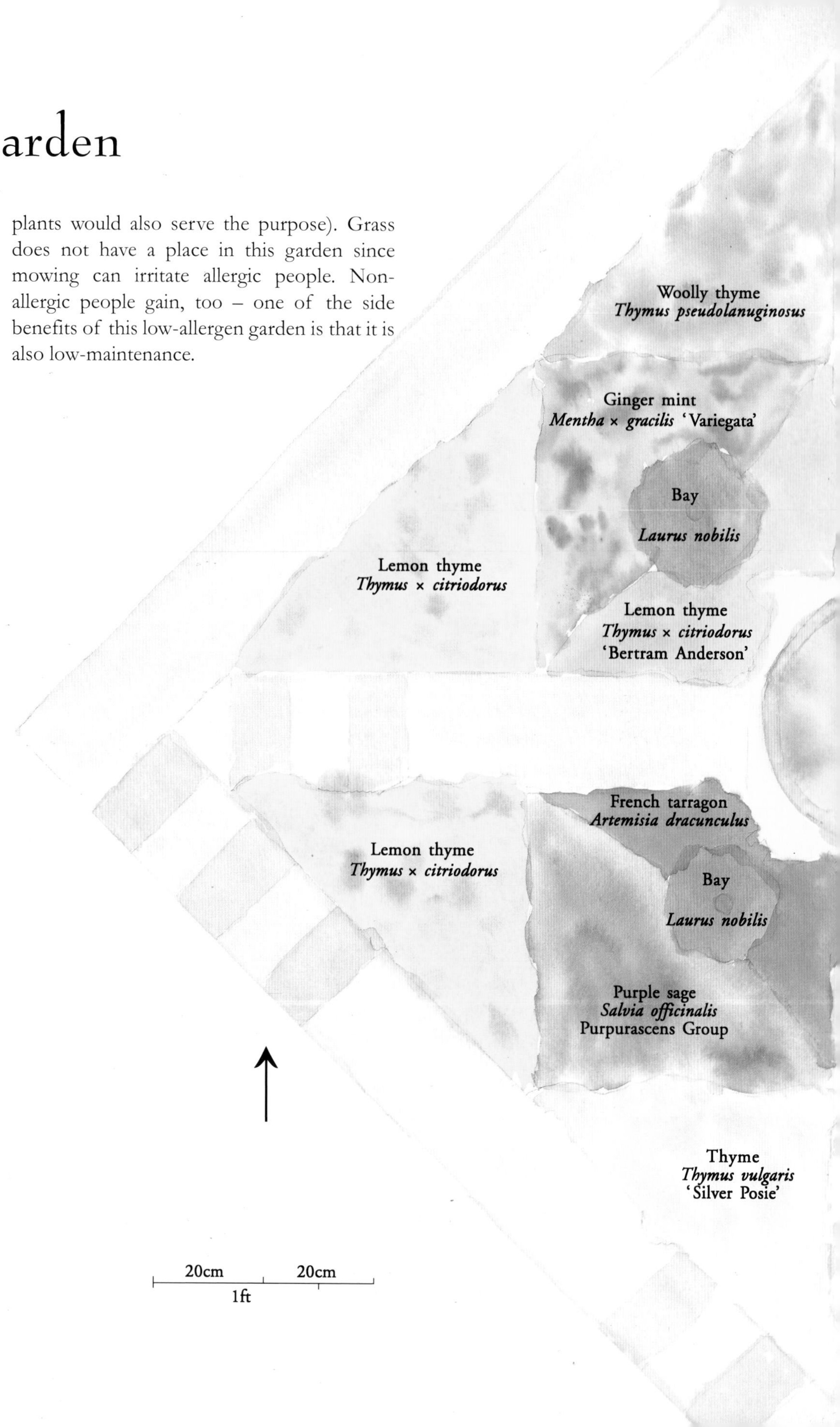

Woolly thyme
Thymus pseudolanuginosus

Ginger mint
Mentha × gracilis 'Variegata'

Bay
Laurus nobilis

Lemon thyme
Thymus × citriodorus

Lemon thyme
Thymus × citriodorus
'Bertram Anderson'

Lemon thyme
Thymus × citriodorus

French tarragon
Artemisia dracunculus

Bay
Laurus nobilis

Purple sage
Salvia officinalis
Purpurascens Group

Thyme
Thymus vulgaris
'Silver Posie'

20cm   20cm

1ft

Woolly thyme
Thymus pseudolanuginosus

Oregano
Origanum vulgare 'Gold Tip'

Bay

Laurus nobilis

Oregano
Origanum vulgare
'Compactum'

Wild strawberry
Fragaria vesca
'Semperflorens'

Variegated lemon balm
Melissa officinalis
'Aurea'

Pot marjoram
Origanum onites
'Aureum'

Oregano
Origanum vulgare
'Compactum'

Bay

Laurus nobilis

Pot marjoram
Origanum onites

Thyme
Thymus vulgaris
'Silver Posie'

RIGHT *Not only does the pot make for variety in the level of planting, it also curbs the lemon balm's vigorous spreading.*

A Herbal Tapestry

Herbal lawns and seats hold a fascination for many gardeners. It has to be said that lawns are notoriously difficult to maintain: they have a tendency to become patchy and are prone to weed invasion. As for seats, these pretty conceits are more pleasant in imagination than in reality, especially if you live in a wet climate.

However, there are many delightful dwarf herbs that deserve some special treatment. And when they are woven into a tapestry, each contrasting detail of form, texture and colour is showcased. This tapestry is not a lawn or carpet in the sense that it is intended to be walked upon regularly. On the other hand, the planting is sufficiently robust to allow the gardener to walk over it for maintenance.

The bed is blanketed in gravel. When preparing for a garden like this it helps to lay a sheet of landscape fabric over the soil surface before covering the garden area with gravel. Landscape fabric is porous, so rain can permeate, but it is sturdy enough to suppress perennial weeds and to prevent other weeds from taking root. Cover the sheet with gravel before planting and,

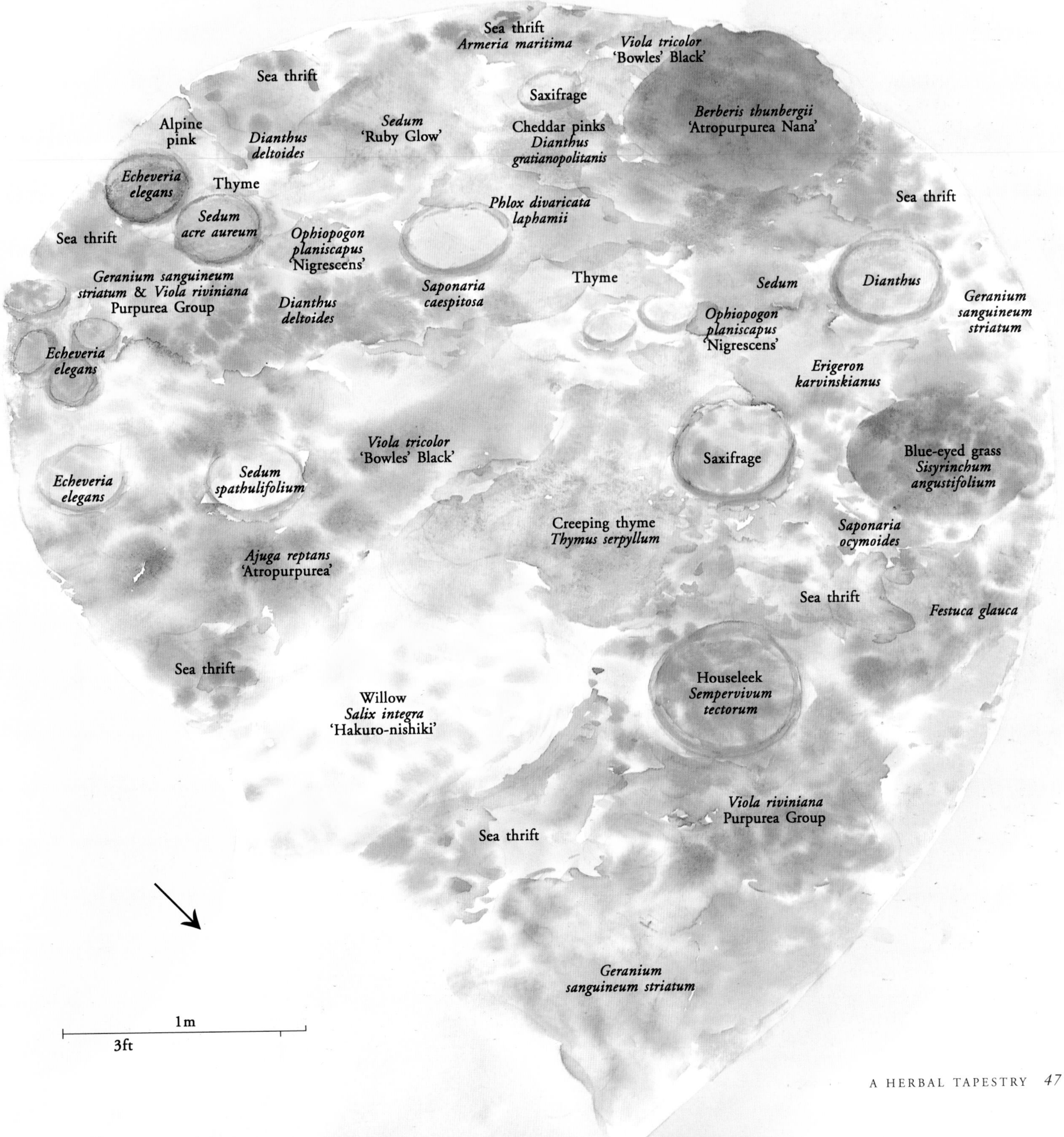

Sea thrift
Armeria maritima

Viola tricolor
'Bowles' Black'

Sea thrift

Saxifrage

Berberis thunbergii
'Atropurpurea Nana'

Alpine
pink

*Dianthus
deltoides*

Sedum
'Ruby Glow'

Cheddar pinks
*Dianthus
gratianopolitanis*

Sea thrift

*Echeveria
elegans*

Thyme

*Sedum
acre aureum*

*Ophiopogon
planiscapus*
'Nigreseens'

*Phlox divaricata
laphamii*

Sea thrift

*Geranium sanguineum
striatum & Viola riviniana*
Purpurea Group

*Dianthus
deltoides*

*Saponaria
caespitosa*

Thyme

Sedum

Dianthus

*Geranium
sanguineum
striatum*

*Ophiopogon
planiscapus*
'Nigrescens'

*Echeveria
elegans*

*Erigeron
karvinskianus*

*Echeveria
elegans*

*Sedum
spathulifolium*

Viola tricolor
'Bowles' Black'

Saxifrage

Blue-eyed grass
*Sisyrinchum
angustifolium*

*Saponaria
ocymoides*

Creeping thyme
Thymus serpyllum

Ajuga reptans
'Atropurpurea'

Sea thrift

Festuca glauca

Sea thrift

Houseleek
*Sempervivum
tectorum*

Willow
Salix integra
'Hakuro-nishiki'

Viola riviniana
Purpurea Group

Sea thrift

*Geranium
sanguineum striatum*

1 m

3 ft

when the time comes to plant, simply brush the gravel aside, make a small slit in the fabric with a sharp craft knife, loosen the soil to make a planting hole and insert the plant through the opening. Brush the gravel back into place around the base of the plant.

Many of the plants chosen for this tapestry have dark, nearly black foliage or flowers: black-leaved bugle, *Ajuga reptans* 'Atropurpurea', *Viola riviniana* Purpurea Group, with inky-purple foliage, *V. tricolor* 'Bowles' Black', with flowers as dark as midnight, and black snakegrass, *Ophiopogon planiscapus* 'Nigrescens'.

Brightening up this somewhat melancholy collection are tufts of Cheddar pinks, *Dianthus gratianopolitanus*, sea thrift, *Armeria maritima*, *Phlox divaricata* subsp. *laphamii, Geranium sanguineum* var. *striatum*, the rock soapwort, *Saponaria ocymoides*, and its cousin, *S. caespitosa*. All of these have flowers in tints of pink. Limpid pools of baby blue come from *Sisyrinchium angustifolium* (called the blue-eyed grass for its tiny gentian-blue flowers) and tussocks of the blue grass, *Festuca glauca*.

Two shrubs, *Berberis thunbergii* 'Atropurpurea Nana' and *Salix integra* 'Hakuro-nishiki', a dwarf willow with variegated foliage marked in pink and white, add some height, as do pots of succulent sedums, *Echeveria elegans* and the common houseleek, *Sempervivum tectorum*.

Pots containing (from left to right) Sempervivum tectorum, Echeveria elegans, *Sedum acre aureum and (behind)* Sedum 'Ruby Glow' *contribute a little height, in this worm's eye-view of a herbal tapestry created from dwarf and rock garden plants.*

Beside the Kitchen Door

For several years the area outside my back door has been a wasteland of tired-looking grass with a few struggling perennials and shrubs. In my hurry to get into the main garden I have avoided paying attention to this sorry space. However, dashing out to the kitchen garden in the rain to pick herbs does not make much sense either. It is time to take matters in hand, and so I have planned a herb garden for myself.

This neglected patch of yard has exactly the right dimensions to contain a small formal herb garden, just big enough for a few shrubby herbs and a rose or two. Fortunately there are no perennial weeds. The area has been turfed over a layer of sand, so when I have sprayed the grass with a herbicide and rotovated it into the soil I should have a good free-draining tilth, well conditioned by the chopped-up dead turf incorporated with the sand and existing topsoil.

The site is against the sunny end of the house, so it bakes in the sun all day. Along one side is a 2m/7ft tall brick and flint wall, a remnant of the old farmyard. This offers me the opportunity to have specimens of white-flowered rosemary and the gilded rosemary, which might not otherwise prove hardy outdoors.

For hedging I have decided upon the small-growing evergreen *Santolina rosmarinifolia* subsp. *rosmarinifolia*. This santolina is of great value as an edging: it roots with extraordinary ease, and a hard clipping in late spring keeps it flowerless and in shape all summer. The clippings can be used for cuttings.

Around the edges where the beds meet the gravel drive I shall plant several varieties of thyme, a bush of purple sage and the narrow-leaved white-flowered sage 'Albiflora'. Lifting and dividing plants in the kitchen garden will give me winter savory, French tarragon, both common and garlic chives, Greek oregano and salad burnet. I must remember to save seed of dill, chervil, rocket, flat-leaved and moss-curled parsley, coriander and the lovely nasturtium 'Empress of India', and to buy seed of miniature bush basil and basil 'Purple Ruffles'. I cannot be without mint, but I shall confine it to the bed beneath the living-room window, where it can clothe the ground at the foot of the incense rose, *Rosa primula*.

I want to keep the central space open, so I shall have only low herbs in the middle beds. All the tall statuesque herbs – angelica, bronze and green fennel and camphor plant – can be planted around the corner, to form a thicket of contrasting foliage shapes and tints.

As a final touch I shall scatter a packet of pot marigold seeds and one of heartsease over the planting to let them come up where they will – which is usually in just the right place.

Flat-leaved parsley & *heartsease pansies,* Petroselinum crispum neapolitanum & Viola tricolor

Thymus herba-barona

Thymus serpyllu 'Pink Chint

Apothecary's rose
Rosa gallica officinalis

White-flowered rosemary
Rosmarinus officinalis albiflorus

White-flowered sage
Salvia officinalis 'Albiflora'

Origanum vulgare 'Compactum'

Purple basil
Ocimum basilicum 'Purple Ruffles'

Santolina rosmarinifolia rosmarinifolia

Moss-curled parsley
Petroselinum crispum

Garli chive
Alliu tuberos

Chervil
Anthriscus cerefolium

Greek oregano
Origanum vulgare hirtum

Flat-leaved parsley
Petroselinum crispum neapolitanum

Dill
Anethum graveolens

Rocket
Eruca vesicaria sativa

Winter savory
Satureja montana

Bush basil
Ocimum basilicum minimum

Chives Allium schoenoprasum

Salad burnet
Sanguisorba minor

Coriander
Coriandrum sativum

French tarragon
Artemisia dracunculus

Thymu serpyllu 'Lemon C

Gilded rosemary
Rosmarinus officinalis 'Aureus'

Gold-variegated sage
Salvia officinalis 'Icterina'

Thymus 'Doone Valle

Heartsease pansies
Viola tricolor

Common thyme

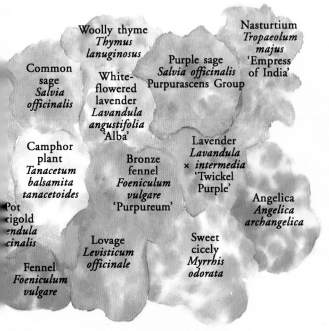

Common
sage
*Salvia
officinalis*

Woolly thyme
*Thymus
lanuginosus*

Purple sage
Salvia officinalis
Purpurascens Group

Nasturtium
*Tropaeolum
majus*
'Empress
of India'

White-
flowered
lavender
*Lavandula
angustifolia*
'Alba'

Camphor
plant
*Tanacetum
balsamita
tanacetoides*

Lavender
*Lavandula
× intermedia*
'Twickel
Purple'

Bronze
fennel
*Foeniculum
vulgare*
'Purpureum'

Angelica
*Angelica
archangelica*

Pot
marigold
*Calendula
officinalis*

Lovage
*Levisticum
officinale*

Sweet
cicely
*Myrrhis
odorata*

Fennel
*Foeniculum
vulgare*

1m	1m
3ft	3ft

Angelica, Angelica archangelica

Moroccan
mint
Mentha spicata
'Moroccan'

Incense
rose
*Rosa
primula*

Nasturtium, Tropaeolum majus *'Empress of India'*

White-flowered sage, Salvia officinalis *'Albiflora'*

Yellow and Purple Accents in a Narrow Border

Iceland poppy
*Papaver
nudicaule*

*Artemisia alba
'Canescens'*

Dyer's
camomile,
golden
marguerite
*Anthemis
tinctoria*

Bronze fennel
*Foeniculum vulgare
'Purpureum'*

Alecost, costmary
Tanacetum balsamita

Heartsease,
wild pansy
*Viola
tricolor*

*Sisyrinchium striatum
'Aunt May'*

Hidcote lavender
*Lavandula angustifolia
'Hidcote'*

Sage
*Salvia officinalis
'Icterina'*

Cotton lavender
*Santolina
chamaecyparissus*

White-flowered rosemary
*Rosmarinus officinalis
albiflorus*

*Lavandula stoechas
pedunculata*

Golden marjoram
Origanum vulgare 'Aureum'

Golden
feverfew
*Tanacetum
parthenium
'Aureum'*

Dill
*Anethum
graveolens*

Pot marigold
*Calendula
officinalis*

Chives
*Allium
schoenoprasum*

Chervil
*Anthriscus
cerefolium*

Purple basil
*Ocimum basilicum
'Purple Ruffles'*

French marigold
Tagetes patula

Thyme
Thymus vulgaris 'Silver Posie'

50cm

1ft   1ft

←

Planning a narrow border requires much more discipline than designing a border for a more spacious site. When working out the scheme, aim to impose a strict rhythm so that the finished planting flows easily from one end to the other. Scale is the first consideration since anything too tall or too squat will make an uneasy interruption. Shapes should be simple, unfussy and well balanced. Colour should be restricted; too broad a palette would appear jumpy, so restrain yourself and limit the harmonies either to one part of the spectrum or to one colour and its complement.

In this border of 1×3m/3×10ft, the central feature is a white-flowered rosemary that will grow to 1.2m/4ft. The other shrubs – lavender, sage and santolina – are lower-growing but have similar rounded shapes and are repeated along the length of the border. The height also changes from front to back, with low-growing herbs to the front and an upright-growing artemisia, fennel and alecost for a backdrop.

There is a chance that the fennel might outgrow the desired height, but this is easily dealt with by simply cutting back the stems as necessary. Just before it flowers, fennel forms the most delightful pale wings at the leaf axils, accentuating the upright habit of the plant. This vertical accent is brought into the middle ground by the spiky foliage of sisyrinchium and chives and spears of lavender flowers.

The bright yellows of French and pot marigolds, Iceland poppies, golden feverfew and marjoram, alecost and *Anthemis tinctoria* are complemented by purple-leaved basil and the mauve flowers of the lavender and chives. The low-key yellow variegations of *Salvia officinalis* 'Icterina' are picked up by the golden marjoram at its feet.

With any luck, *Viola tricolor* will seed itself about, adding its tiny purple, yellow and white flowers to the grey and silver leaves of lavender, artemisia and santolina which underpin the yellow and purple motif of the planting.

The other annuals, especially dill and chervil, should also be allowed to self-sow, but then discreetly weeded. This will soften the mature perennial and shrub planting with a fine dusting of feathery foliage and flecks of colour.

This plan uses plants of small stature. For an even more vivacious display, you might like to try tall-growers from the sunflower genus, such as *Helianthus* 'Loddon Gold' and *H. multiflorus,* with *Inula magnifica* and *Rudbeckia* 'Herbstsonne'. Hem this cloth-of-gold arrangement with equally strident blues, like *Salvia patens* with its lapis lazuli flowers, and top it off with the royal-purple flower wands of *Verbena bonariensis.*

Bright yellow poppies, French marigolds and golden feverfew frame the mauve-purple of Lavandula stoechas *subsp.* pedunculata *in this section of the border. The long, narrow leaves of* Sisyrinchium striatum *'Aunt May' echo the spiky foliage of the lavender bushes.*

A Quincunx of Herbs

Inspiration for knot garden patterns can come from various sources. Some ornamental device nearby may provide the theme – the pattern of brickwork on a terrace, the tracery of a stained glass window. Alternatively, you can turn to designs intended specifically for gardens. As well as the diagrams published in early gardening books, there is a wealth of plans and old engravings to be found in the books and periodicals of the nineteenth and early twentieth centuries.

The knot garden shown here took its inspiration from a herb garden created in 1907 by the great garden designer Gertrude Jekyll, for Knebworth Park in Hertfordshire, the home of the Earl of Lytton. Miss Jekyll's interest in herbs is evident from the catalogue of plants she sold from the nursery at her home, Munstead Wood. She listed 'sweet-scented herbs and shrubs that are associated with the oldest of English gardens'. Together with the beloved lavender, santolina, thyme, rosemary and marjoram, she had *Valeriana phu* 'Aurea' for its golden spring foliage, *Verbascum olympicum,* the woolly grey mullein, a little white-flowered periwinkle that had been collected in Italy, and *Veratrum nigrum,* which in spring has the most dramatic foliage, unfolding its leaves like a silken fan.

The herb garden at Knebworth was in the form of a quincunx – an arrangement of four plants marking the corners of a square, with a fifth placed in the centre. The figure originally described the planting of fruit trees in orchards, as advocated in the seventeenth century by John Evelyn in his *Pomona* (1679).

The design used by Miss Jekyll was adapted to make this herbal quincunx in front of an imposing old house. A large turning-circle became redundant when the approach to the entrance was altered, and some formal garden feature was called for to break up the ocean of gravel. Miss Jekyll's plan indicated rosemary bushes at the four corners and lavender at the centre, with a combination of hyssop, tarragon, thyme and both winter and summer savory to

surround the rosemary, and sage to encircle the lavender. Here the key points of the quincunx are marked by four yew topiary cake-stands and a stone urn. Box edging describes circles around the four yews, and Hidcote lavender outlines the inner circles around the urn. Bushes of *Santolina chamaecyparissus* planted between the cake-stands have grown into soft grey tuffets. The outer perimeter of the quincunx is defined by concentric rings of brick and knapped flint set in the gravel.

On her Knebworth plan Miss Jekyll indicated alecost, marjoram, southernwood, fennel and rue to be used as dot plants in the outer circles. This would have made a garden of subtle contrasts in foliage tints and textures. But when a garden is sited at the entrance to a particularly eye-catching building – like this one, with its warm pink colourwash – flowers make a more

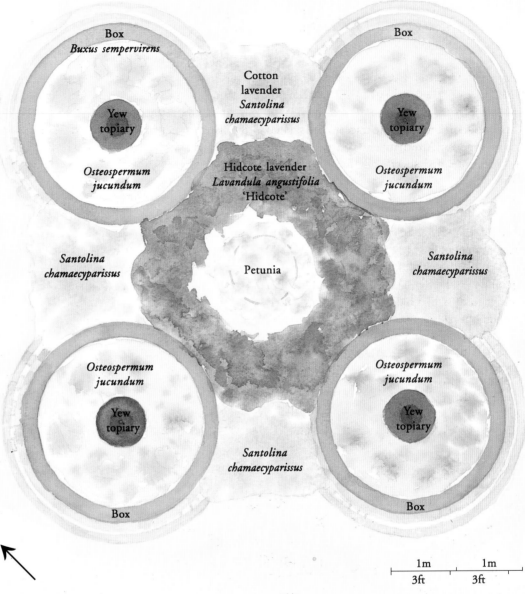

dramatic statement, which in this case is underlined by their scent. During the summer the circles are filled with the pungently fragrant evergreen perennial *Osteospermum jucundum* – with this, the scent is in the foliage rather than the waxy pink petals. The central urn overflows with honey-scented white petunias. As the sun

In this dramatic planting scheme at the entrance to a house painted a distinctive deep pink, wheels of colour spin around a formal central feature.

warms the gravel, the scent of box, lavender and santolina is released. Then, as evening draws in, all the flowers fold their petals as though this part of the garden were closed for the day.

All through the autumn and winter, because of the evergreen topiary and edging and the ever-grey infills, the garden continues to do its job, enhancing the charm of the manor house. Spring brings a different floral display of brightly coloured tulips.

A Golden Border

More than twenty different plants combine to make this border in gold and green, a composition strongly flavoured by the presence of herbs. This is part of a large double border scheme on either side of a gravel path. Across the path the planting begins with shades of pale blue and ends in inky purple; these yellow tints make the perfect complement. Informal in style, the borders are also an exercise in ecological planting executed with a careful eye to colour.

The unity of this garden picture rests not only on the choice of clear yellows for flower colour and leaf variegation, but also on the shared cultural requirements of the plants. This area of the garden lies in the shadow of the house and catches the sun only during the early hours of the day, when it is at its weakest. Many yellow-leaved plants scorch in full sun, so a semi-shaded border suits them admirably. Here the soil is moist and cool, ideally suited to the majority of the plants chosen.

The border banks gently down to a curving gravel path and at its back the lawn sweeps away, dissolving into a meadow studded with apple trees. A cornelian cherry, *Cornus mas*, provides a firm foundation to the planting group, contributing interest throughout the year. During late winter and early spring its naked branches are covered with tiny yellow star-like flowers; the dark green oval leaves set off the shiny red edible fruits which follow the flowering. In autumn, the foliage takes on a warm wine-red hue.

Tall-growing perennials *Euphorbia characias* subsp. *wulfenii*, *Cephalaria gigantea*, the daylilies 'Marion Vaughn' and 'So Lovely', and *Thalictrum flavum* subsp. *glaucum* contribute fleeting yellow flower colour during summer, while the rest of the time their foliage adds an interesting variety of shape and tint.

The true foliage interest, though, comes from

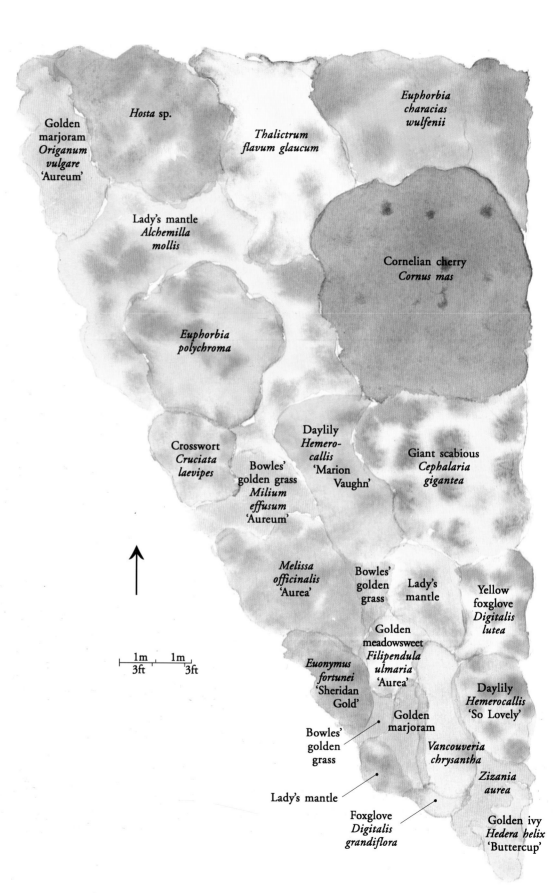

Golden marjoram *Origanum vulgare* 'Aureum'

Hosta sp.

Thalictrum flavum glaucum

Euphorbia characias wulfenii

Lady's mantle *Alchemilla mollis*

Cornelian cherry *Cornus mas*

Euphorbia polychroma

Crosswort *Cruciata laevipes*

Bowles' golden grass *Milium effusum* 'Aureum'

Daylily *Hemerocallis* 'Marion Vaughn'

Giant scabious *Cephalaria gigantea*

Melissa officinalis 'Aurea'

Bowles' golden grass

Lady's mantle

Yellow foxglove *Digitalis lutea*

Golden meadowsweet *Filipendula ulmaria* 'Aurea'

Euonymus fortunei 'Sheridan Gold'

Golden marjoram

Daylily *Hemerocallis* 'So Lovely'

Bowles' golden grass

Lady's mantle

Foxglove *Digitalis grandiflora*

Vancouveria chrysantha

Zizania aurea

Golden ivy *Hedera helix* 'Buttercup'

1m 3ft 1m 3ft

numerous low-growing and carpeting herbs and their ornamental relatives. The golden-leaved ivy 'Buttercup' and *Euonymus fortunei* 'Sheridan Gold', with bright yellow variegation, provide an ever-gold ground, filled in as the growing season progresses with perennial foliage. Yellow-variegated lemon balm, *Melissa officinalis* 'Aurea', golden marjoram, *Origanum vulgare* 'Aureum', and the meadowsweet, *Filipendula ulmaria* 'Aurea', with pure yellow leaves, make the brightest splash. It might have been a temptation to use the lemon balm 'All Gold', which also has pure gold leaves, but the touch of green makes the transition to the acid-yellow flowers of *Euphorbia polychroma* less abrupt. Similarly, it would have been possible to use the variegated meadowsweet, *Filipendula ulmaria* 'Variegata', whose dark green leaves are splashed with gold, instead of the pure yellow *F.u.* 'Aurea'; but the intention was to concentrate the pure tints near the beginning of the border and then have the colour graduate to acid greens and cooler yellows tinged with blue.

The blending of foliage colour is further aided by the smattering of Bowles' golden grass, *Milium effusum* 'Aureum', and lady's mantle, *Alchemilla mollis*, through the foreground and middle ground of the border. These plants are all self-sown seedlings – border plants with this habit are to be encouraged.

Vancouveria chrysantha adds a finishing detail, creeping through the foreground to dangle tiny yellow lantern flowers over the grasses and alchemilla. This vigorous perennial is a native of shady woodlands in the American Pacific north-west regions. The wiry stems are covered in heart-shaped leaves that turn copper-red in autumn – a diminutive echo of the cornelian cherry's seasonal colour.

The plants in this garden border all have similar cultural requirements. They are comfortably at home in the moist, cool, shady conditions, so vigorous maintenance routines are unnecessary. The gardener has only to deadhead the flowers and cut back faded leaves to encourage the growth of fresh foliage.

A Shakespeare Garden

Here's flowers for you
Hot lavender, mints, savory, marjoram;
The marigold that goes to bed with the sun
And with him rises weeping . . .

The Winter's Tale, IV, iii

All these herbs and many more have parts to play – as tokens of love or betrayal, emblems of mortality, signatures of supernatural power – in the works of William Shakespeare. Drawing inspiration from this vast resource, the owner of a garden in the north of France decided to lay out a parterre planted with some of the myriad herbs and flowers mentioned in the plays and sonnets.

Sited on the sunny side of the house, the Shakespeare garden is arranged in a series of three compartments, a square and two rectangles, divided in half by a central path that runs the length of the garden and separated from each other by cross paths. Each bed is contained on three sides by a clipped box edging; the remaining side is left open along the central path to allow the plants to spill over on to the gravel. Little square medallions of knapped flint mark the intersections of the paths.

The formal structure of the garden is repeated in the arrangement of the planting, each bed a mirror image of the one opposite. However, the actual planting is an informal mix of herbal shrubs, perennials, bulbs and self-sown annuals, and while care has been taken to include as many of Shakespeare's plants as possible, a few

LEFT *Plant lists for themed gardens can be drawn from many sources, and this garden-owner has turned to the works of* William Shakespeare. *Twin borders planted with plants and herbs from the plays and sonnets are set in a rural landscape with a traditional Normandy barn and an apple orchard. A grid of paths has been mown in the orchard grass – the natural habitat of Shakespeare's sweet simples.*

strangers have found their way in and been allowed to stay – but only if their colour or scent will add to the garden picture.

The interest of the Shakespeare garden is kept throughout the non-flowering months by the strong foundation of box edging and gravel paths and by clumps of painted sage (*Salvia officinalis* 'Tricolor'), winter savory, lavender, common thyme and ground-hugging woolly thyme. Other shrubby herbs used include *Artemisia abrotanum* and *A. absinthium* (Shakespeare's 'bitter wormwood'), blue- and white-flowered varieties of catmint, and simple pot marjoram. The golden marjoram 'Thumble's Variety' is prominent in the middle beds, making large hummocks of bright yellow; this variety is particularly good for an open position since it does not scorch in bright sun as most pure yellows tend to do. These woody-stemmed plants are cut back to ground level after flowering or in midsummer when they begin to look straggly. This encourages a second flush of foliage to keep the garden looking fresh into the autumn. Wallflowers, *Erysimum cheiri,* and alecost or costmary, *Tanacetum balsamita,* are also given this rejuvenating treatment, the erysimum to prevent it from going leggy, the alecost to ensure a second show of the downy grey-green foliage.

Bottom urges his fellow actors in *A Midsummer Night's Dream* to 'Eat no onions nor garlick; for we are to utter sweet breath.' But despite this injunction Welsh onions and chives are included in this garden, more for their pretty bobble flowers than the flavour of their leaves.

Primroses, cowslips and oxlips have all come out of the hedgerows and into Shakespearean plays and gardens. The flowers of Ophelia's 'fantastic garlands' are well represented – fennel, pansies ('for thoughts'), daisies. Her columbines are there, with canary-yellow double buttercups, *Ranunculus acris* 'Flore Pleno', stippled through the mass of nodding indigo flowers. Attention

to details of harmony and contrast is evident throughout – although some flowers, like the heartsease pansy and pot marigolds, go where they please. Another wayfarer is the annual quaking grass, *Briza maxima,* which has drifted in from another part of the garden. It looks so charming, dangling little papery quills over the path, that it is allowed to remain.

There are many other plants which could be added. Lilies, especially Madonna lilies, daffodils and crown imperials, *Fritillaria imperialis,* all feature in the plays, as do Musk roses, *Rosa × alba, R. gallica* and Damasks (including, of course, *R. × damascena* var. *versicolor,* referred to in *Henry VI* by its common name of York and Lancaster rose). More esoteric references include moss, mistletoe and olives, although given the right conditions these too could be cultivated in a Shakespeare garden.

Salvia officinalis *'Tricolor' and* Nepeta × faassenii

Fennel, Welsh onions and sweet cicely

Columbines and double buttercups

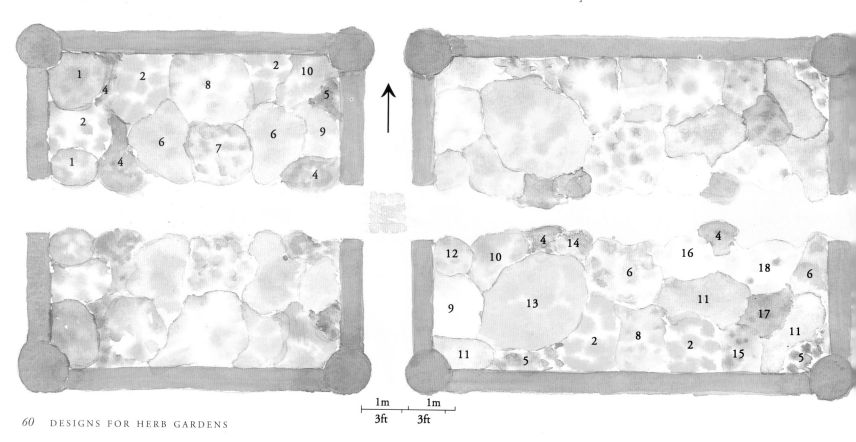

1m   1m
3ft   3ft

BELOW AND OVERLEAF *The ingenuity of the planting scheme for the Shakespeare garden is not immediately apparent. Gradually what at first seems an informal layout is revealed as strictly formal: the plantings are mirror images on either side of the path.*

Artemisia, columbines, alecost and catmint

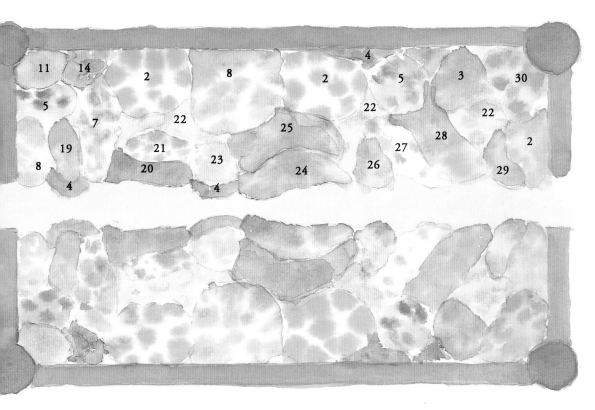

1   *Artemisia abrotanum*
2   Sweet cicely *Myrrhis odorata*
3   Fennel *Foeniculum vulgare*
4   Quaking grass *Briza maxima*
5   Columbines & double buttercups *Aquilegia alpina, Aquilegia vulgaris* & *Ranunculus acris* 'Flore Pleno'
6   Catmint *Nepeta* × *faassenii*
7   Painted sage *Salvia officinalis* 'Tricolor'
8   Pot marjoram *Origanum onites*
9   Wormwood *Artemisia absinthium*
10 Alecost (costmary) *Tanacetum balsamita*
11 *Iris germanica*
12 *Alchemilla erythropoda*
13 Golden marjoram *Origanum vulgare* 'Thumble's Variety'
14 Wallflower *Erysimum cheiri*
15 *Verbascum nigrum*
16 Pinks *Dianthus*
17 *Eryngium plenum*
18 *Geranium renardii*
19 Lavender *Lavandula angustifolia* 'Rosea'
20 Chives *Allium schoenoprasum*
21 Daisies *Bellis perennis*
22 Heartsease pansies, pot marigolds, fumitory & campanulas *Viola tricolor, Calendula officinalis, Fumaria officinalis* & *Campanula persicifolia*
23 Fumitory *Fumaria officinalis*
24 Woolly thyme *Thymus pseudolanuginosus*
25 Winter savory *Satureja montana*
26 Common thyme *Thymus vulgaris*
27 *Nepeta racemosa* 'Snowflake'
28 Calamint *Calamintha grandiflora*
29 Primroses, cowslips & oxlips *Primula vulgaris, P. veris* & *P. elatior*
30 Welsh onions *Allium fistulosum*

Secret Gardens

These knot gardens depend entirely on shrubby plants to define the pattern and fill the spaces with a satisfying variety of leaf shape, texture and colour.

A square within a square and a circle within a square are the motifs chosen for the knots, which are part of a series of secret gardens sited directly behind the house, but screened off from the rest of the garden by tall yew hedges. Grey-leaved santolina marks the perimeter of the square garden, each corner of it dog-legged to make room for a cube of box. The right angles continue with an inner square of box hedging and a box pyramid as the central feature. 'Jackman's Blue' rue infills the square; outside, purple bugle, *Ajuga reptans*, and the dark-leaved violet, *Viola riviniana* Purpurea Group (often to be found labelled incorrectly – as *V. labradorica*) lap up against the feet of the box hedge.

The colour sequence is reversed in the circle knot: box makes the containing square, and box balls are planted in its corners. Mounds of purple *Berberis thunbergii* 'Atropurpurea Nana' are planted in the middle of each side, interrupting the interior circle of grey santolina. A ball of *Santolina pinnata* subsp. *neapolitana* 'Edward Bowles' fills the centre.

Yew hedges border one side of each square and two apple tunnels flanked by beds of Florentine iris and Hidcote and Loddon Pink lavender lead at right angles to the knots. A herbaceous border planted with sedums, Michaelmas daisies, delphiniums, *Geranium sanguineum, Lavatera* 'Silver Cup', night-scented stocks and nasturtiums frames the background.

Rue has a reputation for giving gardeners, or indeed anyone who comes in close contact with it, a nasty blistering rash. Positioned in the centre of a knot, as it is here, it is unlikely to harm anyone but, an alternative could be the sage variety, *Salvia nutans officinalis* 'Berggarten'. It has large, rounded leaves, quite unlike the narrow, pointed leaves of common sage, and their lovely tone of eau-de-nil with a tinge of grey is similar to the blue-green of rue.

Of course, the little purple berberis is not a herb but a much more colourful relative of the common barberry. Except perhaps for a purple sage, it is hard to think of a shrubby herb that would provide the dark masses needed to contrast with the pale tones of santolina.

A garden like this will look rather scalped after pruning in late summer, but regular hard cutting back is what keeps the shrubs looking their best. Left unpruned the santolina will in time turn to a mass of leggy wood. Be severe. Even the oldest plants have surprising regenerative powers, bursting into new growth from old wood as soon as it is exposed to light. Interestingly, where the climate is not too harsh, yew behaves in much the same manner and an old overgrown yew hedge, cut hard back to the trunk, will sprout anew. All this growing takes energy: a nutritious high-nitrogen feed in early spring followed by a summer dressing of general-purpose fertilizer helps to build muscle before the shearing begins.

Santolina is gratifyingly easy to root from shoots trimmed off during pruning. Simply tidy up the cut ends and line the cuttings out in a

A central mound of grey santolina encircled by claret-purple berberis and punctuated by green box domes at each corner makes a colourful display for most of the year.

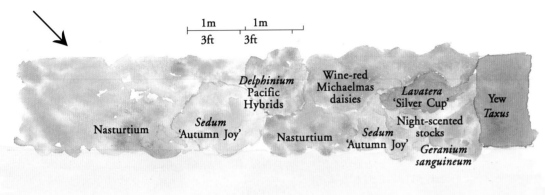

1m | 1m
3ft | 3ft

Delphinium Pacific Hybrids

Wine-red Michaelmas daisies

Lavatera 'Silver Cup'

Yew *Taxus*

Nasturtium

Sedum 'Autumn Joy'

Nasturtium

Sedum 'Autumn Joy'

Night-scented stocks

Geranium sanguineum

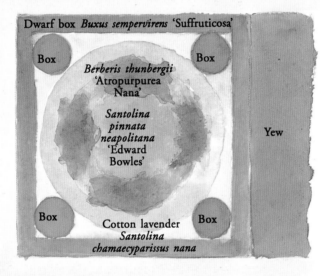

Florentine iris
Iris 'Florentina'

Apple tunnel

Hidcote lavender
Lavandula angustifolia 'Hidcote'

Dwarf box *Buxus sempervirens* 'Suffruticosa'

Box

Box

Berberis thunbergii 'Atropurpurea Nana'

Santolina pinnata neapolitana 'Edward Bowles'

Yew

Box

Box

Cotton lavender
Santolina chamaecyparissus nana

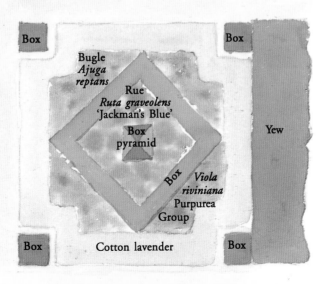

Loddon Pink lavender
Lavandula angustifolia 'Loddon Pink'

Apple tunnel

Florentine iris
Iris 'Florentina'

Box

Box

Bugle *Ajuga reptans*

Rue
Ruta graveolens 'Jackman's Blue'

Box pyramid

Box

Viola riviniana Purpurea Group

Yew

Box

Box

Cotton lavender

corner of the garden where they will not be disturbed. By the end of the following spring they will have rooted and can be transplanted as needed. Clip each new plant over quite hard to encourage bushiness.

Rue and sage are also easy-going when it comes to pruning and taking cuttings. If only the same could be said of box. Cuttings are easy enough to take; after pruning in late summer I line out some of the trimmings behind the pruned hedge. There they sulk for a while but eventually take root – the process has been known to take over a year. Polystyrene seed trays provide an alternative. I have a friend who, each year, lines out neat rows of semi-ripe cuttings in several trays, waters them well and then stows the trays under the greenhouse shelving. She forgets all about them and, miraculously, they root. Really there is no magic about it; it is just that box takes so long to do anything.

Rue, Ruta graveolens *'Jackman's Blue'*

A Bank of Thyme

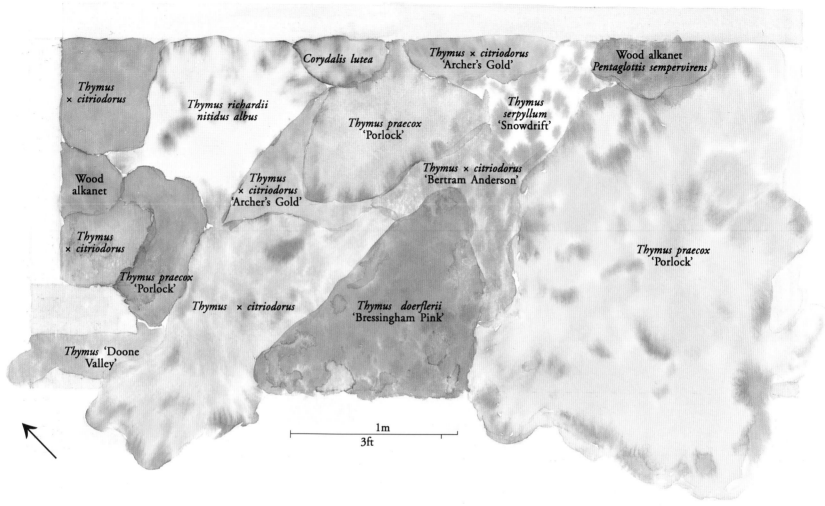

Thymus × citriodorus

Thymus richardii nitidus albus

Corydalis lutea

Thymus × citriodorus 'Archer's Gold'

Wood alkanet *Pentaglottis sempervirens*

Thymus praecox 'Porlock'

Thymus serpyllum 'Snowdrift'

Wood alkanet

Thymus × citriodorus 'Archer's Gold'

Thymus × citriodorus 'Bertram Anderson'

Thymus × citriodorus

Thymus praecox 'Porlock'

Thymus praecox 'Porlock'

Thymus × citriodorus

Thymus doerflerii 'Bressingham Pink'

Thymus 'Doone Valley'

1m
3ft

This garden in Northumberland holds the British national collection of thyme. The collection is cultivated on a raised bed constructed by filling in a south-facing range of brick-sided cold frames, so the plants have all the sun and drainage they need to survive the cold, wet winters prevalent in the north of England. Gardeners who have similar conditions to contend with could follow this example and grow a thyme collection on a bank or raised bed.

Through the ages, the properties of thyme have been held in high esteem. The ancient Greeks regarded thyme as a sacred cleansing herb and branches were burned as incense. Virgil records that it was much valued as a vermifuge and particularly effective against the bite of venomous creatures. To this day it is rubbed on bee-stings to reduce the pain and swelling, which is one reason why bee-keepers have always been advised to grow thyme near beehives. It also used to be recommended that the hives be rubbed with branches of thyme to cleanse them. And one of the earliest garden manuals, *The Gardener's Labyrinth* (1578), suggested that 'the owners of the hives have perfite foresight and knowledge what the increase of yield of honye will be everie yeare, by the plentiful or small number of flowers growing and appearing on the thyme about the Summer solstice.' The bees love thyme flowers, and thyme honey is greatly prized; Greek Hymettus honey has always been especially valued, its rich flavour coming from the cloak of thyme on the mountain where the bees forage.

As a physic, thyme is used by aromatherapists to relieve the aches and pains of rheumatism, sciatica and various strains. An essential culinary herb, and one of the basic ingredients of *bouquet garni*, thyme also aids digestion.

A Silver-blue Sea for a Dry Site

Inspiration for the naturalized planting of this herb-filled corner was found on the sun-baked slopes of the stony hills surrounding the garden. Because the microclimate and soil conditions prevailing within the garden itself are very similar, this approach has resulted in planting that is ecologically appropriate as well as visually satisfying.

The site has a sunny aspect and high walls trap the summer heat. The stillness of the air seems to intensify the bright warmth in the garden. The soil, though moderately fertile, is quite dry; however, winter and early spring rains provide enough moisture to sustain plant growth during the parched summer months. Essentially, it is a sunny, open-ground habitat, and by looking at the native flora of the surrounding French countryside and add-ing a few species from regions with similar habitat characteristics – such as the North American prairies and the dry grasslands of central Europe – a mixed planting requiring little in the way of traditional garden mainte-nance has been created.

Theme plants in this garden are woody-stemmed perennials. *Perovskia atriplicifolia*, commonly known as Russian sage, is found

growing in open stony ground from Tibet to Afghanistan. It has highly aromatic silvery-grey leaves along the upright grey stems, and it flowers throughout late summer, each stem tipped with open spires of lavender-blue. Hyssop is another blue-flowered, woody stemmed herb; it is found in the wild on dry rocky slopes throughout southern Europe and into the eastern regions of Asia. Also flourishing in this bed are two of the thymes, the woolly thyme *T. pseudolanuginosus*, and the creeping thyme *T. serpyllum*, both of which favour an open position in dry stony ground.

Woven into the foundation planting are naturalized clumps of various herbaceous perennials, including the hybrid catmint, *Nepeta* 'Six Hills Giant', and *Eryngium planum*, with many-branched stems tipped with tiny ruffed blue thistle flowers. The globe thistle, *Echinops ritro*, contributes steel-blue drumstick flower-heads in late summer. *Salvia pratensis*, a non-herbal relative of common sage, has greenish bracts that persist after the flowers drop, prolonging the effect of the plant within the scheme. Clumps of the pewter-grey grass *Sesleria caerulea* have colonized the perimeter of the bed and a tall mullein, *Verbascum nigrum*, has seeded itself in the foreground.

All these perennials share similar habitat requirements, and their mutual compatibility means that there is little competition between them for water and available nutrients. In that respect the planting is self-sustaining. Another shared characteristic is that the perennials, with the possible exception of the globe thistle, are comparatively slow to increase. Consequently, apart from the occasional thinning out of the globe thistle, the planting can be left

As the seasons progress, in this garden the colours move from the fresh greens of spring foliage, through clouds of sky-blue and soft mauve flowers in summer, and fade to the tea-stain browns, biscuit and cream of stem and seedhead in late summer and autumn; a self-sustaining garden planting that is beautiful all year round.

undisturbed. Routine lifting and dividing is not required.

Further, many of the perennials flower in late summer, and the plants are commensurately late in developing a dense leaf cover. This gives biennials and annuals, like the blue cornflower, *Centaurea cyanus*, love-in-a-mist, *Nigella damascena*, and clary, *Salvia sclarea* var. *turkestanica*, a chance to colonize.

In summer, as the flowers begin to appear, the silvery green of the garden is transformed to a sea of shimmering blue. This in time will turn to a misty haze as the colour density fades with the flowers, and seed is set and dropped. Then the whole garden can be cut down, any perennial weeds that may have managed to get a foothold can be removed, and the plants can begin their cycle of regrowth.

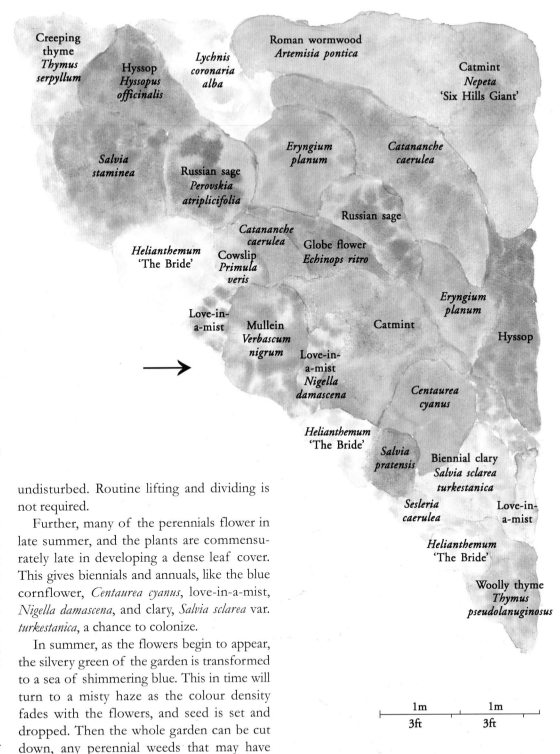

A Movable Feast: Herbs in Containers

Almost any herb can be grown in a pot – good news for those who garden in a confined space, and for cold-climate herb-growers who want to be able to move tender plants to winter shelter. And just about anything that will hold soil makes a suitable container: simple terracotta flower pots, pottery ewers, elegant wooden Versailles cases, fruit punnets, close-weave baskets. You can create an interesting display by simply selecting attractive herbs and putting them into shapely containers.

For something more special, you might like to try creating some herbal topiary. Topiary standards look well planted in large terracotta pots, Versailles cases, urns or half-barrels, and then underplanted with a selection of biennial or small shrubby herbs. Standard lemon verbenas, like the one shown opposite, make an especially attractive feature for the herb garden. Portuguese laurels, bay trees, rosemary and scented pelargoniums also make good subjects for training as standards.

To raise a topiary standard, pot up a rooted cutting in a 10cm/4in pot of general-purpose potting mix, taking care to preserve the growing tip. Position a thin bamboo cane, about twice the height of the cutting, next to the stem, and tie the stem loosely to the cane. The stem should be retied and the cane replaced as the standard gains height. Pot on periodically to the next-sized pot, always being careful to preserve the growing tip or leader. If this is broken side-shoots will develop, and while one of these can be selected to replace the leader, the stem will develop a kink that spoils the line of the mature standard. As the standard grows pinch out any side-shoots along the stem. Feed it

A collection of terracotta pots houses plantings of herbs: feathery fennel with golden grass and gilded honeysuckle; a clump of chives fringed by golden thyme; a collection of different thymes around a little clipped box ball; a cushion of saxifrage; and Viola riviniana *Purpurea Group with bronze fennel and Bowles' golden grass.*

ABOVE *Painted cobalt blue and encrusted with a naive mosaic, this unusual and original container elevates its contents of* Lavandula stoechas *subsp.* pedunculata, *Californian poppies, rue and red orach out of the border and out of the ordinary.*

ABOVE RIGHT *Lemon verbena,* Aloysia triphylla, *is not hardy enough to overwinter in the open garden in a cool climate. Permanently housed in an ornamental pot, it can decorate the summer garden, then be moved to the safety of the greenhouse for winter.*

regularly. When the standard reaches the desired height, pinch out the leader so that the side-shoots develop into branching stems. These should be cut back annually by about one-third. Move tender standards under glass for the winter. Do not water during dormancy. In the early spring, when the stems begin to form leaf buds, prune back the old growth and resume watering and feeding.

The standard lemon verbena shown here is one of four in my garden. They are now five

years old and 1.2m/4ft tall and each spring they burst out in citrus-sweet scented leaves followed by a halo of white flower spikes. I pinch out the first crop of flowers, to encourage leaf and branch, but leave the second flush.

This standard is underplanted with gold-leaved forms of sage, feverfew, marjoram and a gilded thyme – a density of underplanting which means that the pot absolutely must be watered every day, and fed with a balanced liquid fertilizer every three weeks.

A Planting of Pot Herbs

You do not need an excuse to grow herbs in a pot, but the best reason to do so is because space is limited. You may have only a tiny terrace, but still be determined to harvest your own herbs for the kitchen – nothing adds savour like freshly picked mint, parsley or sage. Or you may have a large garden with the herb garden further away than you would like on a dark night or a rainy day and would welcome a handy pot or two within easy reach of the back door. Pots are also a useful way of containing invasive herbs like spearmint that tend to take over a herb patch.

Consider the mature shapes of the herbs when planning the container so that the finished effect is both beneficial to the plant (for instance, will it get enough light or will it be dominated by its trailing upstairs neighbour?) and pleasing to the eye.

Herbs grown in pots should be treated like annuals. In that way, the soil can be replenished each season, and the perennial herbs lifted, divided and thereby reduced in size to suit the limited growing space offered by a container. Do this in late winter or early spring so that the herbs can bulk up to provide plenty of leaf from summer onwards. Superfluous herbs can be potted up and given to friends.

Try to place the pot where the sun can reach it early in the day, but where it will not bake in full heat. Keep an eye on watering – don't overdo it, just make sure it does not dry out. Nutrients are soon washed out of potting compost, so feed regularly with a high-nitrogen fertilizer to encourage plenty of leaf growth; foliar feeds are handy to use for container gardening, and a spray or diffuser on a garden hose makes them easy to administer.

Regular use of herbs for cooking will keep the plants pruned and free from flowers which, if they were allowed to turn to seed, would soon sap the plants' energy.

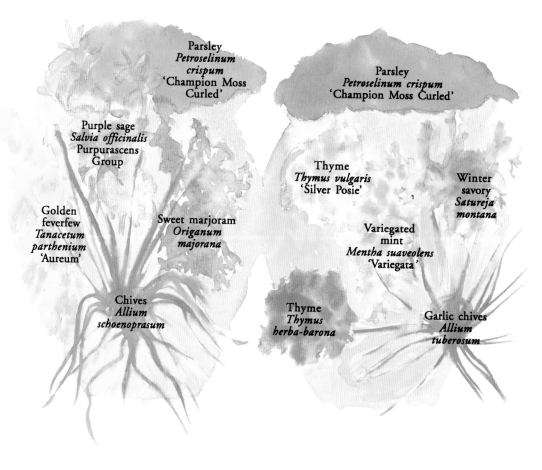

Parsley
Petroselinum crispum
'Champion Moss Curled'

Purple sage
Salvia officinalis
Purpurascens Group

Golden feverfew
Tanacetum parthenium
'Aureum'

Sweet marjoram
Origanum majorana

Chives
Allium schoenoprasum

Parsley
Petroselinum crispum
'Champion Moss Curled'

Thyme
Thymus vulgaris
'Silver Posie'

Winter savory
Satureja montana

Variegated mint
Mentha suaveolens
'Variegata'

Thyme
Thymus herba-barona

Garlic chives
Allium tuberosum

A Pot of Thyme

Typically, creeping ground-covering thymes are grown to do just that – make a spreading carpet of tiny leaves, studded for a week or two annually with white, pink, mauve or purple flowers. Sometimes they are planted to soften the edges of a terrace or in the cracks to interrupt a solid run of paved path or to blur the sides of garden steps with deep treads. But the spreading habit can be turned to a trailing effect if the plants are used vertically to display their variety and versatility.

A strawberry pot offers a perfect opportunity to show off a collection of creeping thymes. There are well over eighty species and varieties of thyme on which to base such a scheme. Here common thyme (*Thymus vulgaris*), common wild thyme (*Thymus serpyllum*), lemon thyme (*Thymus × citriodorus*), caraway thyme (*Thymus herba-barona*) and woolly thyme (*Thymus pseudo-lanuginosus*) have been selected for the variety of their foliage, taste and smell. Thymes with the tiniest round leaves contrast with long and narrow foliage, and the colours range from a glossy rich green to nearly pure yellow, and golden variegated to silver edged. Such a planting makes a noteworthy feature of a group of plants normally given a minor cosmetic role in the garden.

Herbs need good light for at least half the day so place the pot in a suitable position. To plant up a strawberry pot, first ensure there is good drainage. Cover the bottom of the pot with stones or broken crocks. Put in a first layer of potting compost, to come up to the level of the lowest holes. Carefully insert one plant per hole, root first from the outside, and gently jiggle the plant about to shake soil around the roots. Then cover with another layer of potting compost, lightly firming around the roots, and repeat the process to the top of the pot, where the herbs can be planted as normal. Water gently using a fine rose.

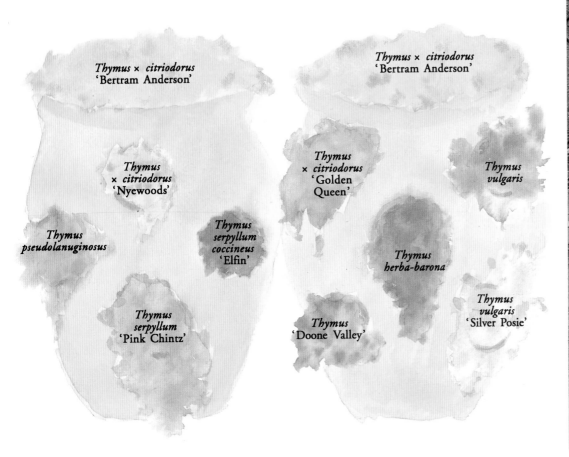

Thymus × citriodorus 'Bertram Anderson'

Thymus × citriodorus 'Nyewoods'

Thymus pseudolanuginosus

Thymus serpyllum coccineus 'Elfin'

Thymus serpyllum 'Pink Chintz'

Thymus × citriodorus 'Bertram Anderson'

Thymus × citriodorus 'Golden Queen'

Thymus vulgaris

Thymus herba-barona

Thymus 'Doone Valley'

Thymus vulgaris 'Silver Posie'

A Scent-filled Scheme

If your passion for growing herbs was born of the sensual pleasure of their scent, then you will of course grow roses. No herb garden should be without the musky, citrusy perfume of the old apothecary's rose, *Rose gallica* var. *officinalis*. Its velvety petals, the colour of mulled wine, were used to make soothing syrups, reviving waters and healing poultices. There are few flowers with such potency.

John Gerard avowed in his *Herball* of 1597 that 'the Rose doth deserve the cheifest and most principall place among all floures whatsoever'. Certainly the allure of other old-fashioned roses, some of which are of as great antiquity as the apothecary's rose, makes them highly collectable. A gardening treatise of 1307 recommended the Alba rose for hedging. Frescoes uncovered at Pompeii depict the autumn Damask, while the York and Lancaster rose named by Shakespeare in *Henry VI* was a summer Damask.

Roses have retained their distinction down the centuries. Dutch flower-pieces, those voluptuous still-life paintings popular during the seventeenth and eighteenth centuries, celebrate the silken beauty of the cabbage rose, *R. × centifolia*. The China rose, which had certainly arrived in Europe from the Orient by about 1781 (and may have been grown in Holland fifty years earlier), added its quality of continuous flowering to the gene pool, allowing the creation of roses which flower more than once each summer. Then there are the Moss roses, so named for the sticky musky moss that covers the sepals, the Bourbon roses whose scent is pure crushed raspberries, the

Pyrus salicifolia 'Pendula' marks the crossing of the gravel paths in this formal quartered garden inspired by the rose garden at Sissinghurst. Rose 'Fantin-Latour', in the bed on the right, has been trained upwards on a tripod frame.

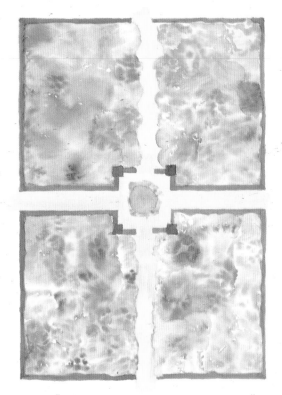

Hybrid Perpetuals, pride of the Victorian gardener, and the Noisettes, which originated in South Carolina.

The great attraction of old shrub roses for anyone designing a mixed herb and flower garden is the ease with which these flowering shrubs blend with herbaceous plants of all kinds. Old roses come in many shapes and sizes, from the neatly compact Damask 'Rose de Rescht' to the lax and lovely striped Bourbon 'Honorine de Brabant'.

The old roses are usually deciduous bushes and some growers maintain that they should be treated as such: their advice is to clip them over after flowering, cutting away the old tired wood, but otherwise to let them grow as they will. This is all fine and good if you have masses of garden space where they can sprawl, but pruning and training do enhance their appearance and promote vigorous flowering.

By cutting out old-flowering wood in the spring and shortening and tying down the longest new growths to half-hoops of hazel ('benders' is their descriptive name) or other supple branches pushed into the ground around the shrub, you can create a shape like an upturned basket that in summer will be smothered in flowers. Alternatively, you can support the main branches with a few sturdy stakes, or train them around a wooden tripod.

Describing the old roses, Vita Sackville-West wrote, 'I could go on for ever, but always I should come back to the idea of embroidery and of velvet and of the damask with which some of them share their name.' It is the texture of velvet that provides the closest analogy for that light-absorbing intensity of hue, ranging from clotted cream through soft flesh-pink and apricot to purple-reds as impenetrable as vintage port.

Vita Sackville-West also admonished her readers to 'take the opportunity of seeing as many of the old roses as possible'. Her own garden at Sissinghurst has long been a place of pilgrimage for gardeners, and her rose garden and writing inspired the design and planting of the garden shown here. (Sissinghurst is also where the basket-training technique was developed.)

The plan of this garden is a traditional quartered rectangle, with each section edged along three sides by clipped box hedging. On the fourth side, along the main path, the plants are allowed to spill over on to the gravel. Where the paths intersect, a silver pear underplanted with *Teucrium × lucidrys* holds court, within a frame of box walls.

Each section is planted with six or seven old-fashioned roses. Gallicas predominate: among them the two striped varieties, Rosa Mundi and 'Camaïeux', crimson-red 'Charles de Mills' and the deeper-tinted 'Tuscany Superb'. Pink-mauve

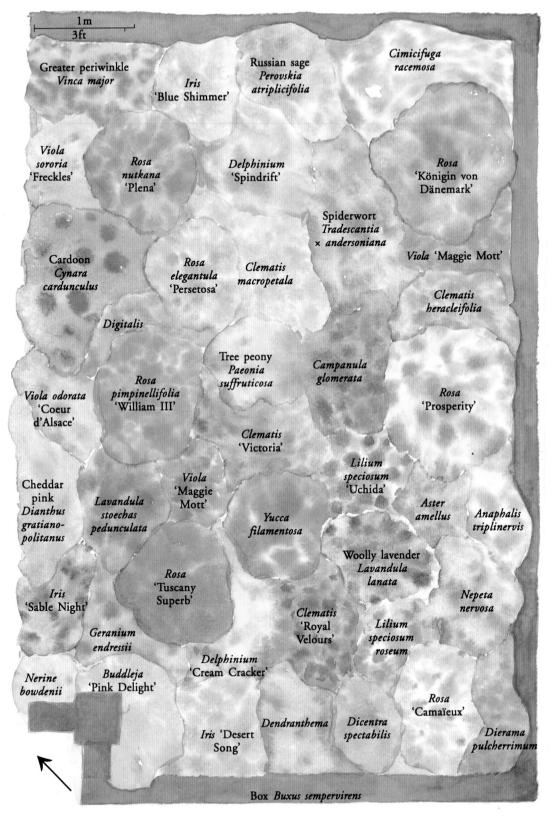

1m
3ft

Greater periwinkle
Vinca major

Iris
'Blue Shimmer'

Russian sage
Perovskia
atriplicifolia

Cimicifuga
racemosa

Viola
sororia
'Freckles'

Rosa
nutkana
'Plena'

Delphinium
'Spindrift'

Rosa
'Königin von
Dänemark'

Spiderwort
Tradescantia
× *andersoniana*

Cardoon
Cynara
cardunculus

Rosa
elegantula
'Persetosa'

Clematis
macropetala

Viola 'Maggie Mott'

Clematis
heracleifolia

Digitalis

Viola odorata
'Coeur
d'Alsace'

Rosa
pimpinellifolia
'William III'

Tree peony
Paeonia
suffruticosa

Campanula
glomerata

Rosa
'Prosperity'

Clematis
'Victoria'

Lilium
speciosum
'Uchida'

Cheddar
pink
Dianthus
gratiano-
politanus

Viola
'Maggie
Mott'

Lavandula
stoechas
pedunculata

Yucca
filamentosa

Aster
amellus

Anaphalis
triplinervis

Woolly lavender
Lavandula
lanata

Iris
'Sable Night'

Rosa
'Tuscany
Superb'

Nepeta
nervosa

Geranium
endressii

Clematis
'Royal
Velours'

Lilium
speciosum
roseum

Delphinium
'Cream Cracker'

Nerine
bowdenii

Buddleja
'Pink Delight'

Rosa
'Camaïeux'

Iris 'Desert
Song'

Dendranthema

Dicentra
spectabilis

Dierama
pulcherrimum

Box *Buxus sempervirens*

'Belle de Crecy' leads into the shell-pink tones of the Centifolia hybrid 'Fantin-Latour'. 'Cardinal de Richelieu' is another Gallica hybrid, as crimson as a cardinal's hat. The pale cheeks of 'Centifolia Variegata' are blushed with streaks of faded strawberry, while the soft pink complexion of graceful 'Königin von Dänemark', an Alba-Damask cross, is unsullied. The Moss roses 'William Lobb' and 'Henri Martin' seem to have doused their petals in vats of vintage claret. The Bourbon roses 'Honorine de Brabant' and 'Mme Isaac Pereire' cast their fruity fragrance on the breeze, while blossoms of the Hybrid Musk roses 'Felicia', 'Prosperity' and 'Cornelia' skitter about in shy shades of peach-pink and rosy apricot. There are varieties of the Scotch burnet rose, *R. pimpinellifolia*, for early flowering, and two species roses, *R. nutkana* 'Plena' and *R. elegantula* 'Persetosa', with russet-coloured foliage and hips in shades of coral, garnet and ruby, continue the colour interest into late summer.

All these myriad reds require careful consideration when appointing the accompanying planting of herbs and ornamentals. If you begin with pure red on a colour wheel and move in one direction, the red becomes warmer and more orange as it approaches yellow; in the opposite direction it becomes cooler and more purple as it turns to blue. Each gradation in either direction needs a different tint of blue, lavender or mauve, pink or cream to complement it. The more crimson a rose is, the bluer its companions can be. If the redness of the rose tends to purple, then work in pale mauves and lilacs or soft creamy yellows and buff colours. In the bed shown in the plan, dusky plum-coloured 'Tuscany Superb', partnered by the dark purple bearded iris

OPPOSITE *The huge felted grey fronds of the cardoon,* Cynara cardunculus, *make a strong contrast to the small flowers and foliage of the surrounding roses,* Rosa nutkana *'Plena', R. elegantula 'Persetosa' and R. pimpinellifolia 'William III'.*

'Sable Night' and the indigo flower-spikes of *Lavendula stoechas* subsp. *pedunculata,* is set off by the sooty-mauve viola 'Maggie Mott' and lavender-pink *of Geranium endressii*. Elsewhere in this garden, porcelain-pale 'Fantin-Latour' is surrounded by the equally subtle colourings of grey and faded mauve *Phlomis italica* and lavender 'Twickel Purple'.

Other colour groupings rely less on harmonizing tints than on playing with contrasts: around powder-pink 'Königin von Dänemark' are baby-blue tradescantia, *Viola* 'Maggie Mott', *Clematis heracleifolia* and white cimicifuga (paradoxically known to herbalists as black cohosh).

Throughout the garden clouds of catmint, pinks and scabious drift in and out between the roses and other flowering shrubs, companion plantings that help to blend the rose colours and give cohesion within the formal plan. The roses themselves are given greater definition by the pruning and training techniques described earlier, and strong verticals are provided by clematis hybrids trained up rustic pole supports.

This spellbinding rose garden is deliberately designed to be of interest only during the summer months. It cannot be seen from the house, and on a fine summer evening a stroll through the garden is rewarded by a visit to this sweetly scented paradise.

In this profusely planted bed, Buddleja *'Pink Delight' and roses 'Madame Lauriol de Barny', 'Reine des Violettes' and 'Madame Isaac Pereire' flourish among generous companion plantings of dianthus, stachys and catmint.*

Herbal Surroundings

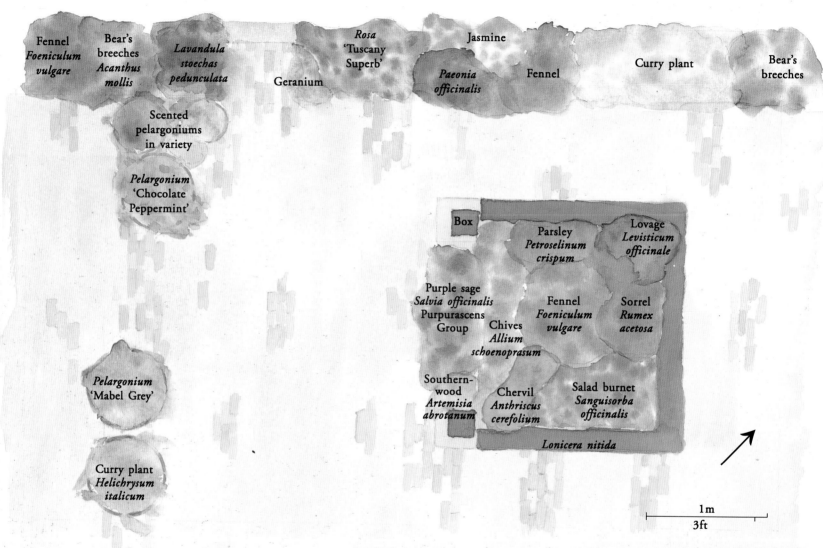

Fennel
Foeniculum vulgare

Bear's breeches
Acanthus mollis

Lavandula stoechas pedunculata

Geranium

Rosa 'Tuscany Superb'

Paeonia officinalis

Jasmine

Fennel

Curry plant

Bear's breeches

Scented pelargoniums in variety

Pelargonium 'Chocolate Peppermint'

Pelargonium 'Mabel Grey'

Curry plant
Helichrysum italicum

Box

Parsley
Petroselinum crispum

Lovage
Levisticum officinale

Purple sage
Salvia officinalis Purpurascens Group

Chives
Allium schoenoprasum

Fennel
Foeniculum vulgare

Sorrel
Rumex acetosa

Southern-wood
Artemisia abrotanum

Chervil
Anthriscus cerefolium

Salad burnet
Sanguisorba officinalis

Lonicera nitida

1m
3ft

Some of the most profound words of gardening wisdom were written by the American landscape architect Thomas Church: 'Landscaping is not a difficult art to be practised only by high priests,' he stated. 'It is logical, down-to-earth and aimed at making your plot of ground produce exactly what you want and need from it.' What was needed in this garden was a way of levelling out the garden area around the house without actually engaging in the tremendous cost and disturbance of earth-moving. The house is built at the top of a slope descending to a shallow ravine, at the bottom of which is a small creek. Clearly, a terrace was needed, and it would have to be fairly substantial – spacious enough to be used as an outdoor room. The decision was made to create an L-shaped area round two sides of the house: one end would be an enclosed terrace screened by high walls and hedges, while the other end, which was left open, projected over the sloping site to form a deck. The transition from enclosed space to open space was further emphasized by laying wooden duck-boarding over the projecting deck platform.

Thomas Church believed in the practical and aesthetic appeal of decks, which he referred to as 'wandering porches', invaluable for 'providing the illusion of spaciousness on a sloping hillside'. He traced their lineage back through the

The small bed carved out of the paving is planted with culinary herbs.

The containers outlining the edge of the deck are currently planted with the ornamental grass Festuca glauca, *but chives would look just as distinctive.*

porches and verandahs of American and British Victorian architecture to the balconies of eighteenth-century Europe. It could be taken even farther back, to the early Renaissance and the enclosed terrace garden of the Palazzo Piccolomini at Pienza and the *giardino segreto* behind the Villa Medici at Fiesole. Both these gardens extend the architectural dynamics of the dwelling into the built landscape, creating a viewing platform from which the distant vista can be regarded as a painting with, as its frame, a 'delicacy of gardens', a terrace planted with sweetly scented flowers and fragrant herbs.

The owner of this garden wanted to have a generous measure of herbs, both useful and ornamental. The terrace includes herbs intended for use (in the small square bed in the centre of the paving) and those planted purely for decoration (in the planting against the house). The owner is a sculptor, so perhaps the emphasis on bold shapes and contrasting forms is not surprising. In the narrow beds beside the house, common fennel, with its mist of bright green foliage, sets off the sculptural leaves of *Acanthus mollis*, once used as a physic to treat sprains and bruises. 'Tuscany Superb' – a showier relative of the apothecary's rose – and *Lavandula stoechas* subsp. *pedunculata* are planted on either side of the door, to make a fragrant entrance which is further enriched by sweet jasmine, red-flowered peonies and the pungent curry plant, *Helichrysum italicum.*

Fines herbes are a combination of parsley, chervil, chives and tarragon, commonly used to flavour chicken, fish and omelettes. What makes the herbs *fines* is that they are freshly picked and chopped; none of them holds its flavour well when dried. Chervil, in particular, seems to lose its aniseed tingle and tastes more of lawn-mowings. All the *fines herbes* except tarragon are to be found in the kitchen square here. Other herbs include lovage, tasting like a cross between celery and tarragon, and salad burnet, which tastes (rather acridly) of cucumber. All of these herbs can be used to enliven green salads.

Pots of scented pelargoniums should be on every terrace where their fragrance can be easily enjoyed. Unless you live in a totally frost-free zone, scented pelargoniums will have to be over-wintered under glass. However, a yearly summer sojourn out of doors will benefit their growth. Repot the plants in the spring; when they reach the largest pot you can handle without too much struggle, refresh the soil by replacing the top 5cm/2in with fresh potting compost. Clear away dead foliage, prune out withered stems and cut back leggy growth to make a tidy shape. Cuttings can be taken in early spring to renew stocks and to make plants to give to friends.

There are dozens of scented pelargoniums to collect. One of the best is the lemon-scented 'Mabel Grey'; she has stiff crinkly leaves and an upright habit, and a mature plant will reach nearly 1.2m/4ft. 'Attar of Roses' and 'Prince of Orange' explain their scent by name. *P.* Fragrans Group has small lobed grey-green leaves strongly scented of pine. 'Acushla' is a new hybrid with tiny oakleaf-shaped, cream-variegated foliage smelling of apples and incense. 'Lady Scarborough' has a similar spicy perfume, with deeply cut leaves and a tendency to legginess that is easily remedied by regularly pinching out growing tips.

The list could get longer, but we should return to the garden, where large pot-grown specimens of 'Mabel Grey', the peppermint geranium, and 'Chocolate Peppermint' march across the terrace.

There is little in the way of actual gardening on the deck but more plants, including herbs, are grown in beds at the foot of the foundations. Mostly these have flowers or foliage in shades of dark purple, wine-red, blue or silver-grey. Among them are common and purple sage, the mourning widow geranium (*G. phaeum*), cotton lavender, fennel and columbine.

Pelargonium *'Mabel Grey'*

Pelargonium *Fragrans Group*

The narrow beds on either side of the door are planted with vibrantly contrasting foliage herbs such as fennel, bear's breeches and Lavandula stoechas *subsp.* pedunculata. *Boston creeper and rose 'Tuscany Superb' clothe the walls and scented pelargoniums stationed in pots break up the brick-paved expanse of terrace, clearly defining separate areas for sitting and strolling.*

Herbal Bedding in a Topiary Garden

The combined talents of an authority on the architecture and gardens of Edwin Lutyens and an inspired and knowledgeable plantsman have led to the creation of the most extensive formal garden made in recent years in England.

The part of the garden considered here, a pair of identical box parterres, lies to one side of the main axis. The tall beech hedges surrounding it offer protection from the strong prevailing winds blowing in off the North Sea, and ensure that the enclosure retains an air of intimacy and tranquillity. They also guarantee that you come upon the garden unexpectedly – a breathtaking surprise that is compounded by the grand scale of the central 'Golden King' holly standards, each about 4.5m/15ft tall, and the solid lines and geometry of the common box edging.

The parterres are planted out each season with a changing cast of annual plants, making the most of contrasts in colour and tone. In this summer scheme, graded from silver-grey to inky purple, the darkest colour is supplied by an oriental herb, purple perilla or beefsteak plant, *Perilla frutescens* var. *crispa* 'Shiso Red', known in Chinese medicine as *Zi su*. It has a mild aniseed flavour, less pungent than that of the 'Purple Ruffles' basil it so closely resembles. By

midsummer it will be nearly 1m/3ft tall and balancing the height of the African hemp plants, *Sparrmannia africana,* grown for the decorative value of their large-lobed leaves and terminal clusters of delicate white flowers.

The infill plants are mixed varieties of verbena, purely ornamental relatives of vervain, *Verbena officinalis. Senecio cineraria* and its filigree-leaf version 'Silver Dust' provide the highlights of shimmering silver amid the pale pinks of the verbena and the dark-wine foliage of perilla. A more conventionally herbal display, that is still extravagantly floral, could be composed of pot marigolds Fiesta Mixed, the short-growing sunflower Music Box or the gaily striped French marigold 'Harlequin', planted with masses of frothy blue larkspur.

To carry the planting theme beyond the confines of the box-edged bedding, pots of perilla and the variegated society garlic, *Tulbaghia violacea* 'Silver Lace', with pale cream-striped grassy foliage and umbels of purple flowers, mingle with tall-growing *Melianthus major,* its leaves pungently scented of burnt chocolate.

Topiary spirals and peacocks grown in pots take the place of stone sculptures. They make a pleasing contrast to the linear arrangement of the hedging and pyramids and furnish this garden room, so that it seems an extension of the house. The sense of unity is reinforced by the brick paving used for paths, steps and edges, which matches the house fabric.

The carefully balanced proportions of this formal garden space makes it a success. Even when the bedding is removed, its integrity remains. Throughout the winter months, when frost burnishes the box and the caramel-brown beech leaves hold fast to the branches of the sheltering hedge, this garden is still beguiling.

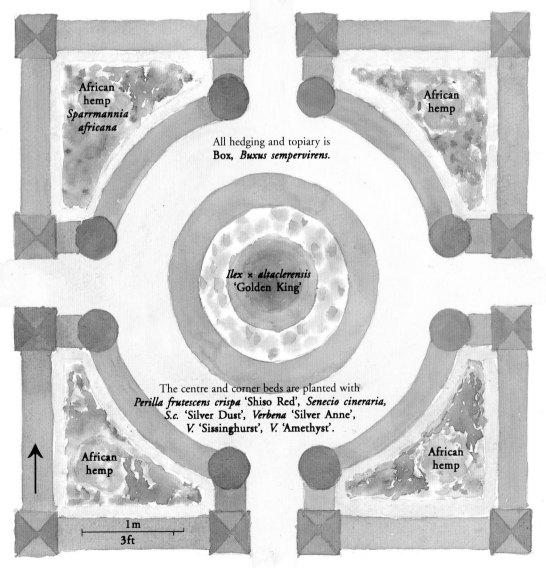

African hemp
Sparrmannia africana

African hemp

All hedging and topiary is
Box, ***Buxus sempervirens.***

Ilex × altaclerensis
'Golden King'

The centre and corner beds are planted with
Perilla frutescens crispa 'Shiso Red', ***Senecio cineraria,***
S.c. 'Silver Dust', ***Verbena*** 'Silver Anne',
V. 'Sissinghurst', ***V.*** 'Amethyst'.

African hemp

African hemp

1 m
3 ft

ABOVE *The dark purple leaves of perilla set off bright verbenas and silver senecio.*

OPPOSITE *One of the pair of ornamental parterres that fills this garden room. Its owners have dubbed it the 'Dutch Garden', in reference to the Edwardian fashion for topiary gardens inspired by the gardens of seventeenth-century Holland.*

Pastel Harmonies

The genus *Allium* provides the gardener with an enormous range of culinary herbs: onions, chives, garlic, garlic chives, Welsh and Egyptian onions and the wild garlic which give the woodlands such unforgettable pungency in spring.

Though any of these could be translated into the ornamental border, their flowers are rather too meek and mild to stand the competition of showier plants. However, the ornamental alliums, with wonderful bobble heads atop long narrow stems, will hold their own in any scheme. In the stretch of border shown here, one of the most handsome alliums, *A. aflatunense,* is grown in close and perfect companionship with the pink-flowered rough chervil, *Chaerophyllum hirsutum roseum.* This chervil is not the same species as the true rough chervil, *C. temulum.* The contrast between the dish-plate flower-heads of the chervil and the globe-shaped umbels of the allium is balanced by the colour harmony of soft pink with pale rosy lavender.

Porcelain-pink hardy *Geranium clarkei* 'Kashmir Pink' and *Saxifraga × urbium* make a pale foam in the foreground. Underpinning the tall stems of the allium and the chervil are the dark blue and white-flowered forms of Jacob's ladder, *Polemonium caeruleum,* a favourite cottage garden plant with a long herbal history. The root was used by English apothecaries to treat ailments of the nervous system, while in the Pacific north-west Native Americans boiled up the entire plant to use as a hair rinse.

As in all good border plantings there are evergreen features to hold the interest during winter months. A bush of box clipped into three tiers is stationed at one end of the border, and several plants of the stinking hellebore, *Helleborus foetidus,* are dotted along its length.

The soft pinks, mauves and blues of this border reflect the pastel colour range that predominates in the common herbal plants. Polemonium caeruleum, Geranium clarkei *'Kashmir Pink',* Allium aflatunense, Chaerophyllum hirsutum roseum *and* Saxifraga × urbium, *widely varying in form, merge in a soft harmony of colour. Gold-variegated box adds a bright note.*

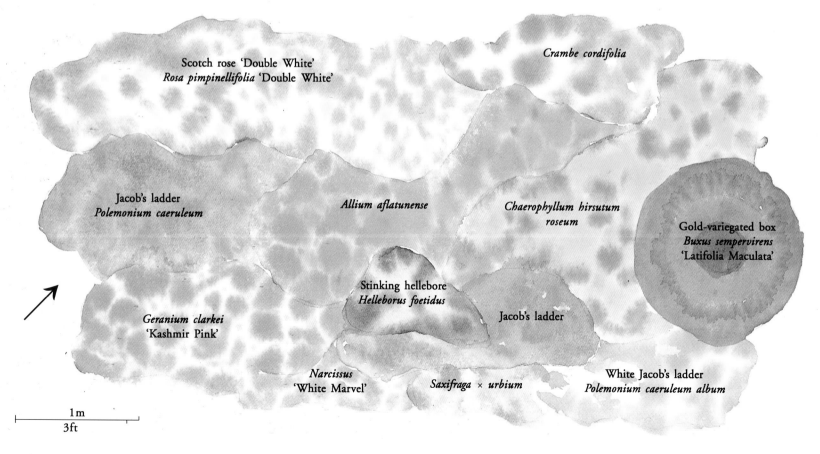

Scotch rose 'Double White'
Rosa pimpinellifolia 'Double White'

Crambe cordifolia

Jacob's ladder
Polemonium caeruleum

Allium aflatunense

Chaerophyllum hirsutum roseum

Gold-variegated box
Buxus sempervirens
'Latifolia Maculata'

Stinking hellebore
Helleborus foetidus

Jacob's ladder

Geranium clarkei
'Kashmir Pink'

Narcissus
'White Marvel'

Saxifraga × urbium

White Jacob's ladder
Polemonium caeruleum album

1 m
3 ft

Grey and Silver Herbs and Grasses

In small crowded beds on either side of the entrance to a half-timbered cottage, there flourishes an impressive array of herbal shrubs, perennials, biennials and annuals, together with a wide range of the ornamental relatives of common herbs, and also some non-herbal grasses. This border is mesmerizing, and a fine example of how herbs can be used as part of a mixed planting.

The plants have been selected for the silver-grey, steel-blue and rust-brown tints of their foliage, but also because they share similar habitat requirements. The finished planting is self-sustaining: the plants support rather than compete with each other and revel in the dry, sunbaked conditions, seeding exuberantly in the free-draining gravel. The density of planting means that there is little scope for weeds to invade. Watering is seldom if ever necessary. All that is required of the gardener is an

RIGHT *Contrasting shapes and leaf forms are played against each other, tall feathery grasses,* Artemisia arborescens *and bronze fennel making a dramatic backdrop to tuffets of low-growing herbs.* Phygelius *'African Queen' adds a touch of sparkling red.*

BELOW *In this planting designed to exploit the dry conditions which so often prevail around a building's foundations, grasses such as* Stipa gigantea *form a matrix for grey-leaved herbs.*

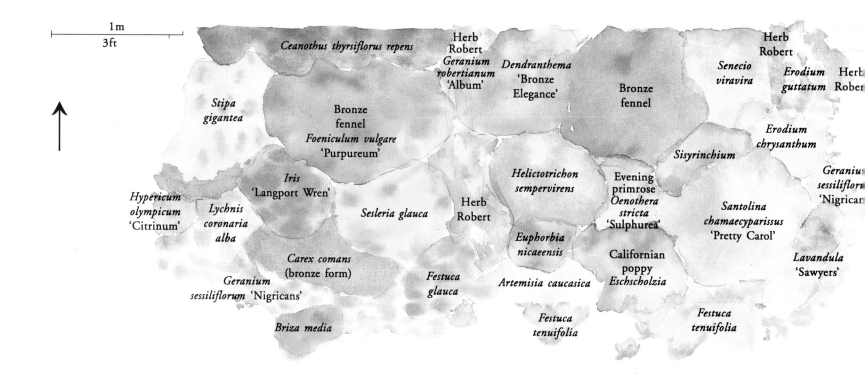

1m
3ft

Ceanothus thyrsiflorus repens

Herb Robert

Geranium robertianum 'Album'

Dendranthema 'Bronze Elegance'

Herb Robert

Senecio viravira

Erodium guttatum

Herb Rober

Stipa gigantea

Bronze fennel

Bronze fennel

Foeniculum vulgare 'Purpureum'

Erodium chrysanthum

Iris 'Langport Wren'

Helictotrichon sempervirens

Sisyrinchium

Geraniu sessiliflora 'Nigrican

Hypericum olympicum 'Citrinum'

Lychnis coronaria alba

Sesleria glauca

Herb Robert

Evening primrose Oenothera stricta 'Sulphurea'

Santolina chamaecyparissus 'Pretty Carol'

Euphorbia nicaeensis

Californian poppy Eschscholzia

Lavandula 'Sawyers'

Carex comans (bronze form)

Geranium sessiliflorum 'Nigricans'

Festuca glauca

Artemisia caucasica

Briza media

Festuca tenuifolia

Festuca tenuifolia

annual tidy-up of faded foliage and a selective thinning of self-sown seedlings.

The informal character of the planting with its soft textures and flowing lines contrasts with the stark geometry of the house. The frothy clouds of foliage are in marked counterpoint to the bold lines of beam against plaster. These two elements – garden and architecture – initially seem independent of each other, but unity is achieved by the colour harmonies which exist between the faded oak beams and off-white of the plasterwork infills and the corresponding silvers, greys, browns and dark black-greens of the leaves.

The plant shapes work in a similar way: strong verticals are counterbalanced by spreading horizontals; broad-leaved, soft-textured plants are partnered by narrow, spiky-leaved subjects. But the limited colour range holds the whole scheme together. Colours that fall outside this range are used sparingly: a touch of coral from the phygelius trained against the

wall, the soft mauve of *Iris* 'Langport Wren' and the flower whorls of *Phlomis italica* make a subtle counterpoint.

In this scheme, as in many other herbal landscapes, the shrubs are the mainstay of the planting. They are, for the most part, evergrey, and their pleasing mounded habit makes a good year-round foundation to a planting scheme. Lavender 'Sawyers' is a relative newcomer and has the palest silver foliage of any lavender. The individual leaves are broad and felted and the flowers are a gentle mauve. The curry plant, *Helichrysum italicum*, and its diminutive subspecies *H. i.* subsp. *microphyllum*, *Artemisia schmidtiana*, *A. arborescens* and *A. alba* 'Canescens' all have pale silver-white foliage and a feathery quality, while *Santolina chamaecyparissus* 'Pretty Carol' is a slightly darker shade of grey, as is *Phlomis italica*. There are also the narrow felted leaves of *Lychnis coronaria alba* and the flat felted leaves of silvery sage, *Salvia argentea*.

Dusted over the silver herb foundation of the borders are other grey-leaved plants – Miss Willmott's ghost, *Eryngium giganteum,* and the pale little catmint *Nepeta sintenisii.* Here and there is the sweet-scented *Oenothera stricta* 'Sulphurea', which is more refined in colour (it is pale cream deepening to apricot) and stature (sprawling to 30 × 45cm/12 × 18in) than the common evening primrose. Perhaps the most delightful traveller is the white-flowered form of herb Robert, *Geranium robertianum* 'Album'. It goes where it pleases and starts life with bright green leaves as finely cut as a lace collar. As the season warms so their colour heats up to a fiery red, and dancing above it all on long trailing stems is a confetti shower of tiny white flowers.

The grasses are mainly steely-blue *Helictotrichon sempervirens* and species of stipa, including *S. gigantea,* which holds its toffee-brown seedheads on 1.5m/5ft stems so that each breeze sends them bopping and bowing.

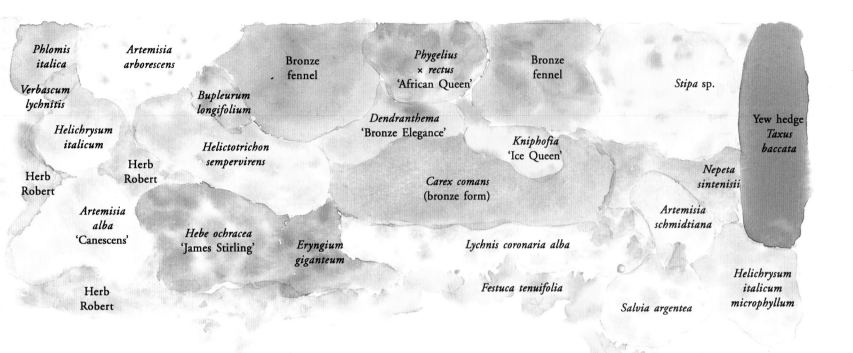

Phlomis
italica

Artemisia
arborescens

Bronze
fennel

Phygelius
× rectus
'African Queen'

Bronze
fennel

Stipa sp.

Verbascum
lychnitis

Bupleurum
longifolium

Yew hedge
Taxus
baccata

Helichrysum
italicum

Dendranthema
'Bronze Elegance'

Helictotrichon
sempervirens

Kniphofia
'Ice Queen'

Herb
Robert

Herb
Robert

Nepeta
sintenisii

Carex comans
(bronze form)

Herb
Robert

Artemisia
schmidtiana

Artemisia
alba
'Canescens'

Hebe ochracea
'James Stirling'

Eryngium
giganteum

Lychnis coronaria alba

Helichrysum
italicum
microphyllum

Herb
Robert

Festuca tenuifolia

Salvia argentea

Festuca tenuifolia expands its territory along the front line, while *Carex comans* (the bronze form) cuts a swathe through the middle ground (it is a relative of the sand sedge, *C. arenaria*, used by German herbalists as a diuretic).

The pale mass of a wall-trained *Artemisia arborescens* is flanked by clumps of bronze fennel, while *Ceanothus thyrsiflorus* var. *repens* hugs the wall on the opposite side of the entrance. In another situation the New Jersey tea, *Ceanothus americanus,* could be used instead, its soft grey foliage and white flowers in perfect keeping with the colour theme. It is hardy to zone 4 and can reach a height of 1.2-1.5m/4-5ft.

As this garden changes through the seasons, the shapes and colours retain their beauty. The moment of true glory comes in early autumn, when the silver shrubs pale to pewter and the bronze grasses mellow to soft chamois gold. With ripening seedheads and spatters of late flower colour, the border fades into an autumn mist.

Santolina chamaecyparissus *'Pretty Carol'*

Evening primrose, Oenethera stricta *'Sulphurea'*

Gold Planting in a Damp Corner

The little circular bed pictured here is planted with gold and variegated herbs, supplemented by a number of ornamental perennials. The effect is cheerful and sunny-looking, and quite transforms what might have been a somewhat gloomy corner.

Care has been taken to match the plants to the site. The bed is at the edge of a pond, where the soil is cool, moist and loamy. The position is shaded for much of the day, so the problem of scorching, which so many yellow-leaved plants are prone to, does not arise. The only problem is that, in these lush conditions, some of the perennials – such as the variegated lemon balm, *Melissa officinalis* 'Aurea', and pineapple mint, *Mentha suaveolens* 'Variegata' – can be thugs, steamrollering less robust neighbours. Their spread has to be checked with a trowel from time to time.

The background planting is of the golden hop, *Humulus lupulus* 'Aureus', the wayfaring tree, *Viburnum lantana* 'Aureum' and the wintersweet, *Chimonanthus praecox*. This is a member of the allspice family, which includes the Carolina allspice, *Calycanthus floridus*. Wintersweet is one of the scented glories of the garden, bearing flowers the size of Lilliputian shuttlecocks but with a potent and delightful fragrance. The leaves are also scented; they appear in early spring after the flowers have faded.

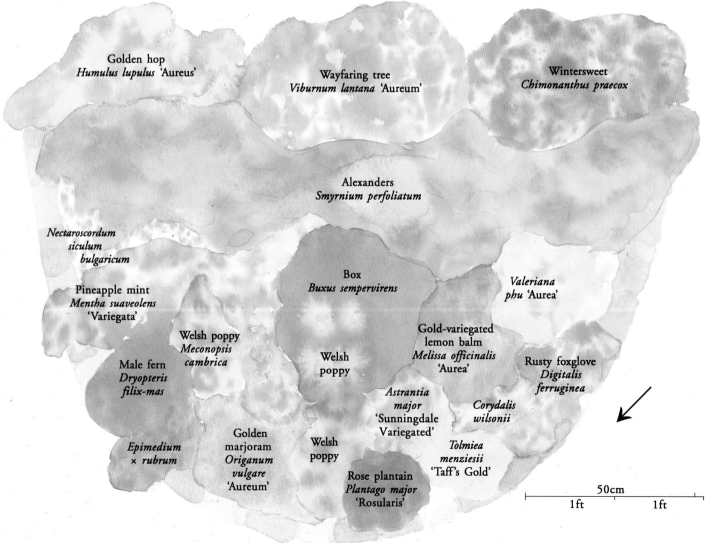

Golden hop
Humulus lupulus 'Aureus'

Wayfaring tree
Viburnum lantana 'Aureum'

Wintersweet
Chimonanthus praecox

Alexanders
Smyrnium perfoliatum

Nectaroscordum siculum bulgaricum

Pineapple mint
Mentha suaveolens 'Variegata'

Welsh poppy
Meconopsis cambrica

Male fern
Dryopteris filix-mas

Box
Buxus sempervirens

Valeriana
phu 'Aurea'

Gold-variegated lemon balm
Melissa officinalis 'Aurea'

Welsh poppy

Rusty foxglove
Digitalis ferruginea

Astrantia major 'Sunningdale Variegated'

Corydalis wilsonii

Epimedium × rubrum

Golden marjoram
Origanum vulgare 'Aureum'

Welsh poppy

Tolmiea menziesii 'Taff's Gold'

Rose plantain
Plantago major 'Rosularis'

50cm
1ft 1ft

An unclipped bush of common box, *Buxus sempervirens,* is planted in the middle of the bed to make an evergreen foliage feature. Between it and the background shrub planting is a bank of biennial alexanders, *Smyrnium perfoliatum.* Its pale green leaves and budgerigar-yellow flower umbels make this relative of black lovage, *S. olusatrum,* an altogether more desirable garden plant. Black lovage is also a biennial but, with a coarser leaf and chunkier flower, it lacks refinement. The Romans introduced it to Britain for use as a stewing vegetable and in the seventeenth century John Evelyn included it in his list of recommended salad greens.

On either side of the box bush are the variegated lemon balm and pineapple mint, with the little lemon-yellow Welsh poppy, *Meconopsis cambrica,* elbowing its way through the foliage. Annual quaking grass, *Briza maxima,* has wandered in from another part of the garden.

Digging their toes into the soil around the cobblestone edging are self-sown seedlings of *Digitalis ferruginea.* They will grow to nearly 1m/3ft and create a screen of bronze-yellow flower spikes. The male fern, *Dryopteris filix-mas,* also pushes up between the stones. It was known to ancient and medieval herbalists as a valuable vermifuge: the root was macerated in honey

water and drunk to purge tapeworms. Another ancient curiosity is the rose plantain, *Plantago major* 'Rosularis', described by Gerard who, 'in company with other apothecaries', saw it growing in the Isle of Tenet (perhaps Thanet?). Although he listed a number of uses for plantains, Gerard felt that the 'ancient writers' greatly overestimated their virtues: their claims were 'not meete to bring into your memory again . . . all of which are but ridiculous toyes'.

When plants are suited to their site — in this case a pondside bed in part-shade — they perform well with only minimal attention from the gardener.

A Physic Garden

The first gardening book written exclusively for women was *The Countrie Housewifes Garden,* published in 1617. The author, William Lawson, wrote from long experience of the correct cultivation of herbs, which were then the mainstay of the garden and of household economy, used in the kitchen to flavour food, in the stillroom to blend cosmetics and preserves, and for physic.

The physic (or medicine) of the time was a blend of rudimentary botanical science, folklore, magic and large doses of common sense. The physic garden, wherein were displayed all the plants an apothecary could need to know, was the forerunner of today's botanic garden, just as Lawson's little book and his subsequent *New Orchard and Garden*, published in 1618, were the antecedents of all the gardening books published today. Lawson gave directions and plans for the shape and planting of herb gardens. He also provided sixteen rules for good garden practices that should be followed by all country housewives – including the injunction to keep an eye on the maids when you set them to the weeding.

The garden shown here belongs to a gentleman's country estate and dates back to the first half of the sixteenth century. However, from 1759 until it was restored during the 1970s, the house had been used as farm outbuildings.

The owners had long been devotees of the cottage garden. A visit to Anne Hathaway's cottage near Stratford-upon-Avon, and the marvellously evocative paintings of cottage gardens by Helen Allingham that illustrate the book *Happy England*, were prime sources of inspiration: both demonstrate the beauty to be achieved by treating house and garden as one unit. Having learned from Gertrude Jekyll the theory of relating the style of the garden to the period of the house, they

turned to William Lawson and his recommendations for laying out a country garden. Lawson's plan showed a rectangular garden divided into six squares, each of which could be allocated to a different design incorporating the plants suited to the purpose. These included a topiary garden, a flower knot garden, kitchen gardens and a fruit garden. There were also walks, a maze, mounts from which to view the garden, beehives and a bowling green; all the features necessary to complete a gentleman's estate.

Here the garden to the front of the house is planted with formal evergreen topiary cut from ivy, holly, box and yew, the four sacred plants of ancient times. Behind the house is a beautiful flower garden, laid out according to Mondrian's principles of composition – an interesting twentieth-century overlay on this purposefully sixteenth-century 'period' garden. A nursery garden (which may one day become a vegetable garden) is organized in rows of raised beds. Finally, there is the physic garden.

One of the farm outbuildings was transformed into an arcaded porch, lending the physic garden the sense of a monastic cloister. Stone boundary walls and the house wall complete the enclosure. The space is rectangular; within this the central beds describe a square sectioned into six wedge-shaped beds by paths laid with coarse sand from the nearby river and edged with local stone. Choosing hard landscaping materials indigenous to the area allows paths and edgings to merge comfortably into their surroundings.

The focal point of this garden is a weeping silver pear 'Bostock', clipped to echo the shape of the arches. It is underplanted with silver-variegated periwinkle, *Vinca minor* 'Argenteo-variegata', a Saxon herb known as 'joy of the ground'.

A weeping silver pear, carefully clipped to an arch shape, provides the centrepiece for the physic garden, a collection of the plants that were the foundation of seventeenth-century domestic economy and medicine.

Artemisia *'Powis Castle'*

Purple bergamot

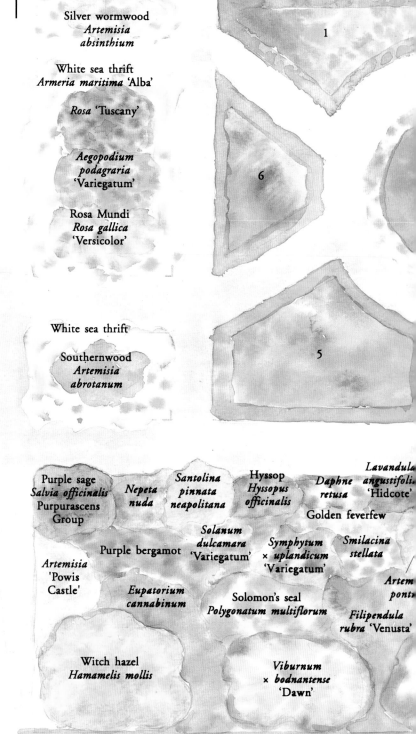

White sea thrift

Silver wormwood
*Artemisia
absinthium*

White sea thrift
Armeria maritima 'Alba'

Rosa 'Tuscany'

*Aegopodium
podagraria
*'Variegatum'

Rosa Mundi
Rosa gallica
'Versicolor'

1

6

5

White sea thrift

Southernwood
*Artemisia
abrotanum*

Purple sage
Salvia officinalis
Purpurascens
Group

*Nepeta
nuda*

*Santolina
pinnata
neapolitana*

Hyssop
*Hyssopus
officinalis*

*Daphne
retusa*

*Lavandula
angustifolia*
'Hidcote'

Golden feverfew

*Solanum
dulcamara*
'Variegatum'

Purple bergamot

*Symphytum
× uplandicum*
'Variegatum'

*Smilacina
stellata*

*Artemisia
'Powis
Castle'*

*Eupatorium
cannabinum*

Solomon's seal
Polygonatum multiflorum

*Artem
pont*

*Filipendula
rubra* 'Venusta'

Witch hazel
Hamamelis mollis

*Viburnum
× bodnantense*
'Dawn'

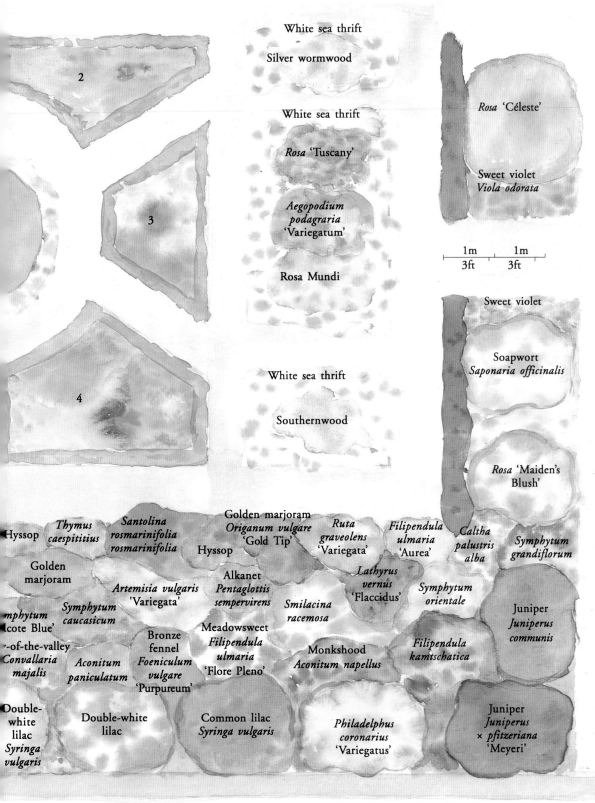

White sea thrift

Silver wormwood

White sea thrift

Rosa 'Tuscany'

*Aegopodium
podagraria*
'Variegatum'

Rosa Mundi

Rosa 'Céleste'

Sweet violet
Viola odorata

2

3

4

White sea thrift

Southernwood

Sweet violet

Soapwort
Saponaria officinalis

Rosa 'Maiden's
Blush'

1m 1m
3ft 3ft

Hyssop

*Thymus
caespititius*

*Santolina
rosmarinifolia
rosmarinifolia*

Golden marjoram
Origanum vulgare
'Gold Tip'

Hyssop

*Ruta
graveolens*
'Variegata'

*Filipendula
ulmaria*
'Aurea'

*Caltha
palustris
alba*

*Symphytum
grandiflorum*

Golden
marjoram

Artemisia vulgaris
'Variegata'

Alkanet
*Pentaglottis
sempervirens*

*Smilacina
racemosa*

*Lathyrus
vernus*
'Flaccidus'

*Symphytum
orientale*

Juniper
*Juniperus
communis*

ymphytum
cote Blue'

*Symphytum
caucasicum*

Bronze
fennel
*Foeniculum
vulgare*
'Purpureum'

Meadowsweet
*Filipendula
ulmaria*
'Flore Pleno'

Monkshood
Aconitum napellus

*Filipendula
kamtschatica*

-of-the-valley
*Convallaria
majalis*

*Aconitum
paniculatum*

Double-
white
lilac
*Syringa
vulgaris*

Double-white
lilac

Common lilac
Syringa vulgaris

*Philadelphus
coronarius*
'Variegatus'

Juniper
*Juniperus
× pfitzeriana*
'Meyeri'

Centre circle *Pyrus salicifolia* 'Bostock', *Vinca minor* 'Argenteovariegata'

Beds 1-6 All edged with *Saxifraga* 'Clarence Elliott'

Bed 1 *Agrostemma githago, Barbarea vulgaris* 'Variegata', *Convallaria majalis rosea, Dictamnus albus, Geranium macrorrhizum* 'Album', *Hyacinthoides hispanica*

Bed 2 *Artemisia abrotanum, Chelidonium majus laciniatum, Convallaria majalis, Dictamnus albus, Filipendula ulmaria* 'Variegata', *Hyacinthoides hispanica, Melissa officinalis* 'Aurea', *Plantago major* 'Rosularis', *Salvia sclarea*, violas

Bed 3 *Aconitum napellus, Artemisia dracunculus, Borago officinalis, B. pygemaea, Galega orientalis, Linum perenne, Origanum onites, Pulmonaria, Stachys macrantha, Tanacetum vulgare* 'Silver Lace'

Bed 4 *Aconitum napellus, Borago officinalis, Galega orientalis, Hyacinthoides hispanica, Linum perenne, Origanum onites, Pulmonaria, Stachys macrantha, Tanacetum vulgare* 'Silver Lace'

Bed 5 *Aconitum napellus, Barbarea vulgaris* 'Variegata', *Borago officinalis, Digitalis ferruginea, Galega orientalis, Hesperis matronalis Lathyrus aureus, Linum perenne, Origanum onites, Origanum vulgare* 'Aureum', *Pulmonaria, Tanacetum vulgare* 'Silver Lace'

Bed 6 *Foeniculum vulgare, Lilium* spp., *Ruta graveolens, Tanacetum parthenium*

As a refreshing change from the ubiquitous box edging, the central beds are edged with pink-flowered *Saxifraga* 'Clarence Elliott' (*S. umbrosa* var. *primuloides*), a dwarf relative of London pride. Another edging, now not so commonly seen in English gardens, but still used in the southern United States, is *Armeria maritima* 'Alba', the white-flowered sea thrift. Here it has been used around the perimeter beds, which are planted with old roses, a variety of white-flowered herbs and the white-variegated ground elder.

As Gerard pointed out in his *Herball*, published in 1597, sea thrift was commonly found in gardens 'for bordering up beds and banks, for the which it serveth very fitly'. But he also noted that 'Their use in Physicke as yet is not knowne, neither doth any seeke into the Nature thereof, but esteeme them onely for their beautie and pleasure.' A comment like this marks a pronounced change in attitudes. The earliest herbals, compiled at a time when gardens were regarded as purely functional, had been practical guides to plants and their uses. By Gerard's time gardens had begun to be made with an eye to pleasure, and herbals were including some plants simply for their aesthetic value.

The plants grown in the physic garden beds here have a wide variety of supposed properties – as medicines, as dyestuffs, for making charms or weaving magic spells and, most sinister of all, as poisons.

It is alarming how many of our common herbs and flowers have the potential to cause illness, even death: foxglove; lily-of-the-valley; *Cyclamen purpurascens* (with the curious rustic name of sowbread). Every part of monkshood or aconite, *Aconitum napellus*, is lethal. Corncockle has poisonous seeds, and the sweet-scented *Daphne mezereum* flower becomes a murderous orange berry. All parts of the laburnum – wood, bark, roots and leaves – are

Beds edged with vivid pink saxifrage and white sea thrift contain herbs grown for both practical use and ornamental effect.

toxic, but the poisons concentrate in the black seed that ripens when the graceful yellow panicles have faded. *Mandragora officinarum*, commonly known as mandrake, was believed to be so deadly that human hands could not harvest it, and dogs were used to drag the screaming root from the ground. Then there is *Prunus laurocerasus*, from which was brewed *aqua laurocerasi*, cherry laurel water. It may sound pleasant enough and was used beneficially by apothecaries, but it also had fatal applications. *Atropa belladonna* – the deadly nightshade – hardly needs describing.

The fabled poison garden of the ancient King Attalus of Pergamum, stocked with 'Aconites, Henbane, Hellebore, and plants hardly admitted within the walls of Paradise' might equally have been a physic garden, for the kingdom was dedicated to Aesculapius, the god of medicine.

So if you wish to make a physic garden, especially if you have small children, do take the trouble to research the potential danger of the plants you intend to include. That is one of the reasons why herbals were and still are being written. Any library should be able to provide you with an up-to-date reference book. In the United States gardeners can also check with their county extension officers.

Common garden flowers had their practical uses, too. Bluebell bulbs are toxic when fresh, but the gooey liquid produced from bulb, stem and leaf has a more prosaic value: it was used during Elizabethan times to starch the stiff lace ruffs that were the height of fashion. Bookbinders also used it as paste.

Dictamnus albus was the false dittany of the old herbals, but we know it today as burning bush. It was made into distilled water and used as a cosmetic and in soothing nerve tonics such as 'Solomon's Opiate' and 'Hyacinth Mixture'.

The greater celandine, *Chelidonium majus* was known as poor man's iodine; if you snap its stem, it secretes a marigold-yellow juice that is effective at taking the itch out of insect bites. Use it thoughtfully, however, because it

leaves a stubborn stain on skin.

Stachys officinalis, commonly known as bishopswort, was once regarded as a cure-all for everything from the common cold to hysteria and was believed to protect against malign supernatural forces. Alkanet, *Alkanna tinctoria*, is little known nowadays, but was once much in demand as dyer's bugloss, because the root when macerated yields a red colourant. This was used throughout Europe by unscrupulous vintners to deepen the colour of substandard port. It otherwise served to impart a red colour to fabrics and cosmetics and to stain wood, especially oak and mahogany.

Provided that you take care where you site

The physic garden herb collection continues in the beds along the surrounding walls, where tall Filipendula kamtschatica, Philadelphus coronarius 'Variegata' and lilacs make a backdrop for lower-growing herbs.

the poisonous specimens, all of these flowering herbs could easily be moved into the flower garden, but it is fascinating to see them growing together in the setting of a physic garden; and, after contemplating the plants themselves, it is pleasant to spend a few hours leafing through an old herbal, wondering at the myriad uses that our ancestors had for so many 'common or garden' plants.

A Sunken Garden with Raised Beds

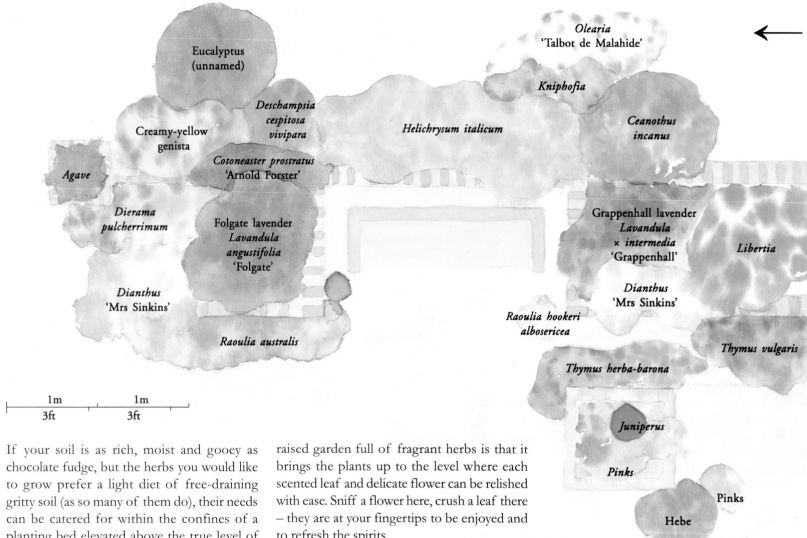

Olearia 'Talbot de Malahide'

Eucalyptus (unnamed)

Kniphofia

Deschampsia cespitosa vivipara

Helichrysum italicum

Ceanothus incanus

Creamy-yellow genista

Cotoneaster prostratus 'Arnold Forster'

Agave

Grappenhall lavender *Lavandula × intermedia* 'Grappenhall'

Dierama pulcherrimum

Folgate lavender *Lavandula angustifolia* 'Folgate'

Libertia

Dianthus 'Mrs Sinkins'

Dianthus 'Mrs Sinkins'

Raoulia hookeri albosericea

Raoulia australis

Thymus vulgaris

Thymus herba-barona

Juniperus

Pinks

Pinks

Hebe

1m 1m
3ft 3ft

If your soil is as rich, moist and gooey as chocolate fudge, but the herbs you would like to grow prefer a light diet of free-draining gritty soil (as so many of them do), their needs can be catered for within the confines of a planting bed elevated above the true level of the site. Alternatively, your own approach to the physical actitivity of gardening may be influenced by the ease with which you can plant, hoe and so on. Raised garden beds are accessible to gardeners in wheelchairs or whose movement is otherwise limited. Besides, even the youngest back gets tired after a marathon weeding session.

Raised beds satisfy all sorts of demands made by herbs and by the gardeners who grow them. However, the greatest attribute of a raised garden full of fragrant herbs is that it brings the plants up to the level where each scented leaf and delicate flower can be relished with ease. Sniff a flower here, crush a leaf there – they are at your fingertips to be enjoyed and to refresh the spirits.

It is delightful to rest, on a still summer evening, on a sun-warmed garden seat surrounded by herbs alive with late-foraging honeybees and butterflies. This is just the opportunity offered by the inviting oak bench in this garden which combines the advantages of a sunken garden with those of a raised bed. The warm brick walls trap the herbal scents, holding them on the still air, while the raised beds make the plants easy to reach.

The garden was created by excavating into a shallow slope, less than 1m/3ft high, and then digging farther down to emphasize the depth. The spoil from the excavation was then banked up around three sides to create raised walkways in the style of the seventeenth century.

On the lowest level, the topsoil was completely removed. This revealed the sandy subsoil and provided the starved, sharply drained semi-alpine conditions so many creeping herbs enjoy. Brick-walled raised beds about 45cm/18in high were created around the footings of the terrace retaining walls and filled with sharp-draining compost.

Behind the bench, and planted into the beds that edge the terrace, *Helichrysum italicum* sends down a shower of gold. With silver foliage pungently scented of fenugreek, cumin and asafoetida, its common name could hardly be anything other than curry plant, though some may know it as false licorice.

To this is added the intoxicating perfume of the white-flowered daisy bush, *Olearia* 'Talbot de Malahide', a frost-hardy evergreen that should be in every seaside garden, and the invigorating snap of resin and citrus from the blue-grey foliage of a young gum tree, a eucalypt grown from seed.

Lavenders 'Grappenhall' and 'Folgate' and the clove-scented pink 'Mrs Sinkins' are planted on either side of the bench, while the gravel at its foot is shot through with any number of creeping thyme varieties and colonies of self-sown pinks that have arrived from other parts of the garden.

Other plants whose contribution is purely ornamental are *Raoulia australis* and *R. hookeri* var. *albosericea* – making dense mats of grey and chartreuse-green – kniphofia and angel's fishing rods, *Dierama pulcherrimum*.

Retaining walls in a raised garden offer the opportunity to grow some graceful weeping varieties of common shrubs. To the right of the bench is a weeping form of *Ceanothus incanus*; *Cotoneaster prostratus* 'Arnold Forster' is to the left beneath a graceful ornamental grass, *Deschampsia cespitosa* var. *vivipara*, also known as 'Fairy's Joke' – the joke being that the plume-like seedheads are actually little plantlets that take root wherever they drop.

The microclimate of a sunken garden offers keen gardeners the opportunity to grow plants that would ordinarily require a good deal of cossetting. Brick-built raised beds also help, because heat retained by the brickwork during the day is given off like central heating

in the evening, while sharp drainage prevents water settling and freezing round the roots. Prostrate rosemary can often be a touchy subject, but this is just the sort of situation it would enjoy. *Boronia citriodora*, a Tasmanian native, makes a small shrub less than 1m/3ft high, more sweetly scented of lemons and oranges than any plant I know; it too would do well in such a snug corner. *Cymbopogon citratus*, lemon grass, is another herb I would grow here; the chopped leaves complement fish and chicken dishes and in Bahrain are used to make a refreshing herbal tea. It can be bought fresh from oriental food markets, with the base of the stems neatly trimmed. Look for ones that have retained the top of the root base, plunge them into moist compost and

With the setting sun bathing the garden in a golden afterglow, the full fragrance of the herbs surrounding the bench is released, the warmth of their perfume enhancing the serenity of the garden.

keep them well watered. The roots will soon shoot again and it can be grown on.

Sink gardens, either the genuine old stone sort or contemporary versions in weathered cast concrete, offer another chance to grow small herbs that would benefit from being raised above the scrum: plants like *Micromeria thymifolia*, a tiny tussock of minuscule scented leaves, little pincushion dianthus, various houseleeks and bonsai-sized junipers are just a few of the miniature herbs that can be used to make mini-landscapes.

A Herb Potager

The publication in 1699 of John Evelyn's *Acetaria: a Discourse on Sallets* heralded a sea-change in dietary trends. For generations it had been believed that fresh fruit and raw vegetables were detrimental to health. The result was that, as Evelyn pointed out, scurvy was rife in many countries, including the New World colonies, and widespread in England. As he further explained, experiment showed that 'raw Sallets and Herbs have been found to be the most soveraign Diet', efficacious in expunging that 'Cruel Enemy'.

Acetaria included chapters on the design and planting of gardens and the raising of flowers and rare plants, as well as one deliriously dedicated to 'Stupendous and Wonderful Plants'. Chapter 20 described all one needed to know about the composition of a salad: how to gather the leaves (and in what sort of basket), in what type of dish to serve the salad, what kind of salt and pepper to use, and the proper preparation of a dressing.

This herbal potager would meet with Evelyn's exacting specifications. Designed to provide salad greens and herbs for a hotel kitchen, it is made to a traditional plan: four squares with their inner quarters sectioned off by narrower paths to create four separate beds. The planting of this working garden, although highly ornamental, is none the less schematic.

The inner beds are edged with lavender, a pair with 'Royal Purple', one with 'Munstead' and one with 'Loddon Pink'. The centre of each square is planted with a different leaf herb: moss-curled parsley makes a thick shag carpet in one, flat-leaved Italian parsley fills its neighbour. Tarragon and dill are found in the remaining two squares. The purple and green chequerboard makes a delightful centrepiece for the surrounding L-shaped salad-leaf beds where the culinary imagination is really let loose on all that the herbal kingdom has to offer.

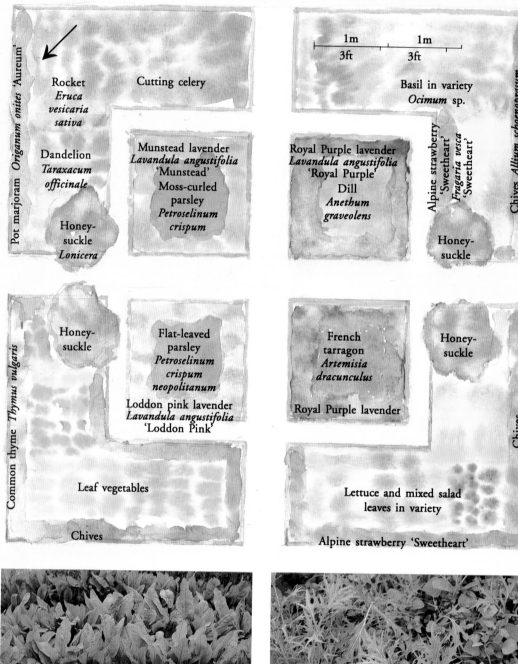

Sorrel

Japanese mustard 'Mizuna'

One entire bed and part of another are devoted to growing different types of basil, from the incense-scented holy basil, Kha Prao (*Ocimum tenuiflorum*) from Thailand, to the best culinary variety, 'Genovese'. 'Lettuce-leaved' basil is a good choice to use whole in mixed salads, as are 'Green Ruffles' and 'Purple Ruffles', because the broad crinkly leaves hold a dressing so well. 'Cinnamon', 'Lemon', 'Horapha' (anise-flavoured) and 'Spice' are good for curries and oriental stir-fry dishes. Tiny-leaved bush basil (*O. basilicum* var. *minimum*) forms tight domes of shining jade-green, so, apart from its kitchen virtues, it makes neat formal edgings.

The remaining beds are devoted to a catholic selection of vegetables grown for their young leaves. There are Oriental leaf vegetables, including several of the brassicas with a warm mustardy savour. Arugula or rocket, from the Mediterranean, has a pungent meaty taste (Gerard's *Herball* says that this herb inspires lust and promotes virility). There are lettuces in variety, and two types of dandelion for blanching to make tender leaves. Leaf celery, also called cutting celery or smallage, is grown for flavouring stock and to use in salads. Chives, thyme, alpine strawberries and golden marjoram are used as edgings.

Edgings of lavender give permanence to a garden mainly composed of annual herbs.

Evelyn's list of thirty-five 'sallets' included spinach, corn salad (lamb's lettuce), land or American cress, salad burnet, sage and sorrel. These greens can be sown in place of the basil once it is over, while some varieties of oriental cabbage, like 'Michihili', can be grown under cloches for winter harvesting.

Nasturtiums also featured on Evelyn's list. I would add the little heartsease viola, violets (which have a pleasing heat), and pot marigolds – and don't forget the chive flowers!

A Potpourri Garden

This garden, as fragrant as it is attractive, is designed for a sunny townhouse courtyard, and planted to provide flowers and foliage for potpourri. Its jasmine-covered arbour, tucked into the corner, offers a vantage point from where to savour the sweet scents. The walls capture the fugitive perfumes which in a more open setting would disperse on the breeze. Low box hedging encloses the central bed and imposes a structured ground plan on herbs that tend to be floppy and wispy. Allow the camomile, thyme and marjoram at the corners to creep over the gravel path, softening the geometry of the floral carpet.

Roses, here trained on trellis attached to the walls, are an essential ingredient of the potpourri garden, their petals forming the base of most mixtures. Choose from the strongly scented species that hold their fragrance well when dried. The climbing rose 'Zéphirine Drouhin' is one of the best for a small space because it is thornless, not overly vigorous and tolerates some shade. Its only weakness is a propensity to mildew and blackspot, but early and regular spraying with a fungicide before the buds break will keep disease at bay. The semi-double flowers are bright pink and are borne all through the summer. Like other Bourbon roses, such as 'Madame Isaac Pereire', 'Zéphirine Drouhin' has a fruity raspberry scent. Damask roses, such as 'Gloire de Guilan' and 'Professeur Emile Perrot', are spicily scented. Hybrid Musks, such as 'Buff Beauty' and the old apothecary's rose, *R. gallica* var. *officinalis*, have strong fragrance and rich colours for potpourri. White roses are best avoided because the dried petals look like shreds of old paper.

Planted beside a path, lavender releases its fragrance as you brush past. It is the only flower, other than the rose, that keeps its scent when dried without needing a fixative such as powdered orris root. *Lavandula × intermedia* Old English Group makes a large bush, so for a small area choose the low-growing *L. angustifolia* 'Hidcote', which is neater,

has a richer colour and is just as pleasantly scented.

In the narrow beds beneath the climbing roses, mixed plantings of annuals and perennials are colour-themed: deep purples and mauve-pinks of sweet sultan, sweet violets and heliotrope and the pale froth of sweet woodruff, night-scented stocks and mignonette; muted colours recede, blurring the edges and helping the space seem larger. If this

is not a consideration, then warm-coloured flowers like pot marigolds, multi-coloured nicotiana, bright yellow perennial wallflowers and red valerian could be used to provide perfume and vivid colour in the garden and the potpourri bowl. But avoid too much height around the edges, or the effect will be claustrophobic.

Foremost among the plants to harvest for

Rosa 'Zéphirine Drouhin'

Rosa 'Zéphirine Drouhin'

Heliotrope, sweet sultan & sweet violets *Heliotropium peruvianum, Amberboa moschata &Viola odorata*

Lemon thyme *Thymus × citriodorus*

Pinks in variety

Lemon verbena *Aloysia triphylla*

Apothecary rose *Rosa gallica officinalis*

Sage *Salvia officinalis* 'Tricolor'

Iris 'Florentin'

Golden marjoram *Origanum vulgare* 'Aureum'

Dwarf box hedging *Buxus sempervirens* 'Suffruticosa'

Scented pelargoniums in variety

Rosemary *Rosmarinus officinalis* 'Tuscan Blue'

Bay *Laurus nobilis*

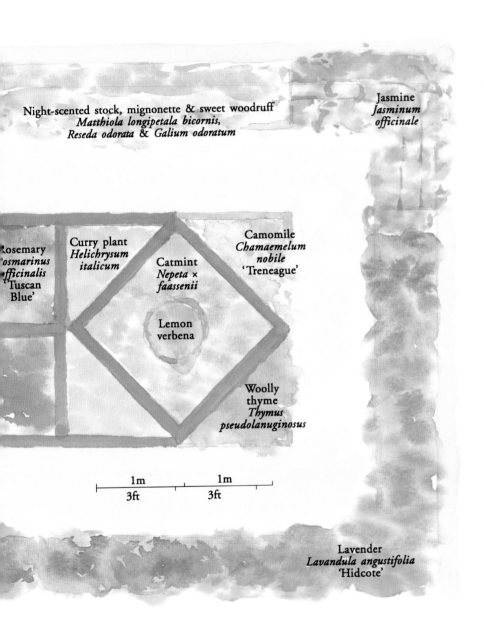

Night-scented stock, mignonette & sweet woodruff
Matthiola longipetala bicornis,
Reseda odorata & Galium odoratum

Jasmine
Jasminum
officinale

Rosemary
Rosmarinus
officinalis
'Tuscan
Blue'

Curry plant
Helichrysum
italicum

Catmint
Nepeta ×
faassenii

Camomile
Chamaemelum
nobile
'Treneague'

Lemon
verbena

Woolly
thyme
Thymus
pseudolanuginosus

1m   1m
3ft   3ft

Lavender
Lavandula angustifolia
'Hidcote'

Iris '*Florentina*'

their aromatic leaves is the lemon verbena, *Aloysia triphylla* (*Lippia citriodora*), which is grown here as a standard to punctuate the centre of each diamond of box. On one side it is surrounded by the heady scent of pinks, on the other by blue *Nepeta* × *faassenii* with grey aromatic leaves. Scented pelargoniums, the tender *Pelargonium crispum, P. tomentosum, P.* 'Attar of Roses' and *P.* 'Mabel Grey', are planted in pots and overwintered indoors.

Powdered orris root, used to stabilize the scent of potpourri, is made from the dried rhizome of the Florentine iris; you won't want to grind your own powder (it is easily obtainable), but do include the plant in such a scheme. The flowers are exquisite – shimmering silvery mauve – and smell delicious. Also, the soft grey-green sword-like leaves look well with the stiff branches of rosemary: choose 'Tuscan Blue' for its vibrant blue flowers.

Gather the flowers and leaves for potpourri on sunny mornings, mix them gently, and allow them to dry slowly in an airy, shady room before adding any fixative. To boost the perfume, add sweet spices and scented essential oil to the dried and blended ingredients. Bowls filled with fragrant petals and aromatic leaves gathered from the potpourri garden will remind you of the sweet smells of summer – stir them by hand as you pass by to arouse the scent.

Simple Serenity in a Secluded Bower

Bamboo is probably the single most useful herb in cultivation in the world. In Chinese herbal medicine the leaves of species within the genus *Phyllostachys* are used fresh or dried as a diuretic and to relieve fevers and inflammation. Throughout the Far East the young stem shoots are used as a vegetable, and since time immemorial the sturdy mature canes have been part of the technology that helped to establish the great civilizations of China and Japan.

To gardeners, in the West as well as the East, bamboo offers a chance to incorporate some of the most aesthetically pleasing architectural plants into a herbal landscape. They range in size from compact plants around head height to towering stems of more than 7.5m/ 25ft, and have a huge variety of leaf shape and stem colour. Another of their attributes, and one which is often overlooked, is the soothing music created by the soft rustle of the foliage as it is stirred by a light breeze. We are often told how the play of water in fountains and rills adds life to a garden. Sir George Sitwell wrote in *On the Making of Gardens*, '. . . sounds which repeat themselves, such as the bubbling of a fountain, the cawing of rooks, the song of the cuckoo, strike a note of peacefulness . . .' I would add to this list of calming sounds the sigh of bamboo.

The meditative tranquillity of bamboo sets the theme for this green herbal bower, where a screen of *Phyllostachys nigra* var. *henonis*, underplanted with lily-of-the-valley and the hardy *Geranium* 'Johnson's Blue', forms the end of a pergola covered in *Laburnum × watereri* 'Vossii'. The pergola runs around the perimeter of the garden. It was designed to provide a shady walk around a sunny and exposed site, with the bamboo arbour creating a cool retreat. In keeping with this, the plants beneath the bamboo are natives of woodland scrub and thrive in dry shade. Other plants that would tolerate the dry shade under bamboo are periwinkles, ferns and the yellow archangel, *Lamium galeobdolon*. The box-edged beds beneath the laburnums are filled with plants chosen for their soft foliage and ephemeral flower colour – filmy green sweet cicely, white columbines (seedlings of *Aquilegia vulgaris)*, wild strawberries and *Aruncus dioicus,* another Chinese herbal plant, also favoured in Japanese gardens for the strong foliage and delicate airiness of the sinuous flower racemes.

An earthenware pot holds aquilegias and a single plant of *Polygonatum multiflorum*. Commonly known as Solomon's seal, this was said by the sixteenth-century herbalist John Gerard to be 'good to seale or close up green wounds'.

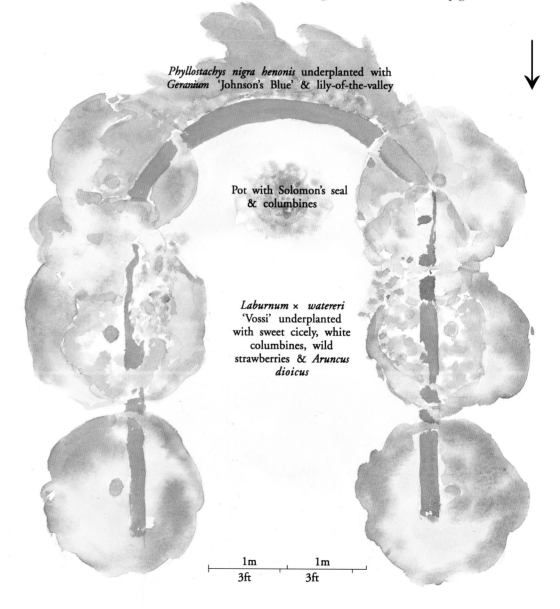

Phyllostachys nigra henonis underplanted with *Geranium* 'Johnson's Blue' & lily-of-the-valley

Pot with Solomon's seal & columbines

Laburnum × watereri 'Vossi' underplanted with sweet cicely, white columbines, wild strawberries & *Aruncus dioicus*

1m	1m
3ft	3ft

He also described a North American species with '. . . leaves long, nervous, and very greene and shining . . . vulgarly named *Polygonatum virginianum'*. Perhaps not the plant to choose for a tranquil setting.

The light, well-drained soil and open position of this garden make it ideal for growing bamboos. They are shallow-rooting and can be grown in the thinnest soils but the best growth is achieved with generous annual feeds of a general-purpose fertilizer and a thick mulch of rotted compost.

Phyllostachys is one of the least invasive bamboos and offers a wide variety of stem colour. The variety used here will reach 7.5m/ 25ft in height. It is one of the black bamboos, although its stems remain green where those of its smaller relative *P. nigra* (growing only to 3.5m/12ft) emerge as bright green and age to midnight black. *P. n.* 'Boryana' becomes blotched with brown. Among other colourful members of the genus, *P. vivax* 'Aureocaulis' is striped emerald-green and canary-yellow; *P. aurea* 'Holochrysa' is pure yellow; *P. viridiglau-cescens* is rich grass-green, and *P. aurea* 'Variegata' has such pronounced variegation that the young leaves appear to be nearly pure white.

Once the plants are established they require little cultivation. Water regularly during the first year following planting, and thereafter rely on mulch to conserve moisture around the roots. Feed annually with a general fertilizer. As the clumps mature cut away older stems and carry out any thinning during the autumn or late winter, to avoid damaging new growth as it emerges in spring to early summer.

A Colour Wheel

All the most appealing garden qualities of herbs are assembled in this magnificent herb garden. In leaf and flower the plants display an abundant variety of form and texture, as well as conveying their primary message of colour. There is scent in abundance, and nectar for the honeybees.

The garden is laid out on a sunny slope, with the planting sweeping up and away from the house and terrace vantage point. The plan is geometric and the use of colour controlled, but the actual planting is relaxed and informal. The beds are laid out as concentric rings divided by gravel paths. Colour is deployed around the circles so that the tints are graded from soft pastel pinks, yellows and blues to violet, magenta, maroon and deep pink. The inner beds, radiating from the central focal point of a sundial set in a camomile carpet, are planted with soft blues. The intention was to create a visual sensation of depth, as though the garden site were concave; this optical illusion is strengthened by the convex contour of the yew hedge running along the top of the slope and framing the round garden.

In the colour wheel garden, herbs, used alongside purely ornamental plants, contribute both to the colour harmonies achieved through juxtaposition of tints and also to careful contrasts of form, shape and texture. In this section of the wheel the velvet-grey foliage of Stachys byzantina *'Big Ears' makes a spreading mat. Behind are fuzzy spheres of* Santolina chamaecyparissus. Sedum alboroseum *'Mediovariegatum', with yellow flowers, makes a low mound, while* Ruta graveolens *'Jackman's Blue' forms another block of solid bluegrey and provides an almost shiny texture that contrasts with the matt surfaces of the neighbouring plants. In counterpoint to the low, hummocky shapes, yellow iris, pink lupin 'La Chatelaine' and* Phlomis russeliana *supply spiky verticals.*

Clouds of blue-flowered catmint, *Nepeta × faassenii*, underpin this central planting. Lavender (*Lavandula stoechas* subsp. *pedunculata*), bugle (*Ajuga reptans*), sage, both common and purple-leaved (*Salvia officinalis* and *S. o.* Purpurascens Group), tiny-flowered violas like 'Belmont Blue', 'Arkwright's Ruby', 'Nellie Britton' and velvety purple-black 'Bowles' Black', the variegated thyme 'Silver Posie' and rosy-mauve lamiums are just a few of the many flowering herbs that thread their way through the blue mist of nepeta blossoms.

Another section of the wheel focuses on soft pinks that tend towards violet. *Phuopsis stylosa* 'Purpurea', which has deeper-coloured flowers than the species, is grown with chives, the chive flower umbels echoing the spherical flowerheads of the phuopsis in both shape and colour. Lupin 'The Chatelaine', its flowers bicoloured pink and white, grows nearby, as does the oriental poppy 'Patty's Plum', its petals the colour of faded mauve silk. Pink columbines (*Aquilegia vulgaris*), buff-coloured foxgloves and a soft lilac-pink iris complete the palette.

'E.C. Buxton', a fine yellow-flowered form of dyer's camomile (*Anthemis tinctoria*), a soft yellow iris the colour of a canary bird, the yellow-variegated sedum *S. alboroseum* 'Mediovariegatum', the creamy yellow foxglove *Digitalis lutea*, golden marjoram and yellow-variegated sage represent the opposite end of the spectrum. These yellows are carefully chosen for their relative coolness and lack any hint of red in their make-up.

While the leitmotif of this garden is colour, the play of contrasts in the foliage form and texture keeps the planting intact before and after the main flowering period. For example, when the chive and phuopsis combination is not in flower, the grassy green blades of the little onion are a perfect foil for the shiny green ruffs that clothe the stems of its partner.

Ever-grey foliage from herbs such as *Santolina chamaecyparissus* and *S. pinnata* subsp. *neapolitana* 'Edward Bowles', common sage, lavender in variety, and curry plant (*Helichrysum italicum*) give form all the year round. Threaded through the plantings are perennial greys like lamb's ears (*Stachys byzantina*), *Artemisia ludoviciana* 'Silver Queen', *A.* 'Powis Castle' and *Ajania pacifica*. Another component consists of soft creamcoloured plants like the variegated obedient plant, *Physostegia virginiana* 'Variegata', and *Phlox paniculata* 'Norah Leigh', with white-variegated leaves. These pale colours are used not only to provide continuing interest but also to aid the transition of one colour planting into another.

Walking around this herb garden — weaving around and between the beds along the gravel paths — is an almost overwhelming experience. Each circumnavigation brings more colour combinations and foliage contrasts into view, and you feel you must explore every angle and enjoy each successive picture. But a rose-covered arbour and a simple bench provide restful vantage points: one looking up the slope of the garden and one looking down. From either of these quiet places it is possible to absorb the view and savour the delicious perfumes of the garden.

At the height of summer much of the scent is provided by the old shrub and English roses deployed throughout the garden. These are placed carefully within the colour framework: soft pinks from 'Ballerina', 'Fantin-Latour', 'Sharifa Asma'; warmer pinks from 'Marguerite Hilling', 'Felicia', 'Lucetta'; butter-yellow 'Leverkusen'; wine-red 'William Lobb', 'Tuscany Superb', 'Mme Isaac Pereire', 'William Shakespeare'; cherry-pink-striped Rosa Mundi, marking the transition into the duskier pink of *Rosa glauca* and the richer tones of 'Cymbeline', 'Mevrouw Nathalie Nypels' and 'Bloomfield Abundance'.

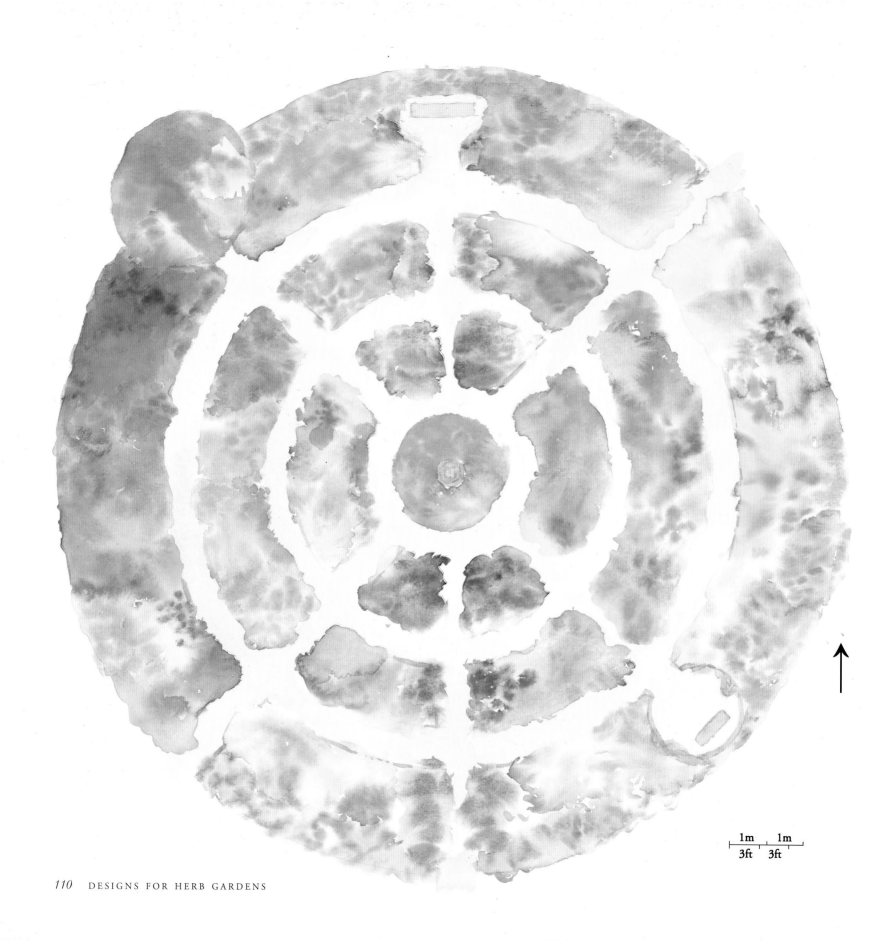

1m   1m
3ft   3ft

Divided into concentric rings around a circular camomile lawn, beds of herbs and ornamental border plants are harmoniously grouped in a scheme that makes the most of subtle flower and leaf colour. If you imagine the garden plan as a clock face and move around it counter-clockwise from six o'clock, the colour sequence starts with pale blues, pinks and creams, merges into blues, lilac and violet with dots of yellow, peaks at midday with magenta and crimson and more blue, and winds down to deep maroon and burgundy and then to deep rosy pinks. The photograph above shows a view of the garden looking from the magenta-pink side across the garden to the blues, purples and yellows.

Suggested herbs and ornamental plants for a similar colour wheel are:

Pale pink and buff *Aquilegia vulgaris, Argyranthemum* 'Mary Wootton', *Digitalis purpurea* 'Sutton's Apricot', *Geranium sanguineum* var. *striatum, Saxifraga* × *urbium*

Blue, mauve and lilac *Centaurea montana, Eryngium maritimum, Geranium* × *magnificum, Lamium maculatum, Lavandula angustifolia, Lavandula stoechas* subsp.

pedunculata, Nepeta × *faassenii, Polemonium caeruleum, Scabiosa* 'Butterfly Blue', *Scabiosa caucasica* 'Clive Greaves', *Thymus serpyllum, Thymus vulgare, Veronica spicata, Viola* 'Belmont Blue'

Cerise, crimson and scarlet *Centranthus ruber, Dianthus* 'Old Clove', *Dicentra spectabilis, Lupinus* 'Inverewe Red', *Lychnis coronaria, Monarda* 'Cambridge Scarlet', *Rosa* 'William Shakespeare', *Stachys macrantha* 'Rosea'

Purple and rose pink *Achillea millefolium, Atriplex hortensis* var. *rubra* 'Cerise Queen', *Lupinus* 'The Chatelaine', *Phlox paniculata* 'Franz Schubert', *Salvia officinalis* Purpurascens Group, *Sidalcea malviflora* 'Rose Queen', *Verbena bonariensis*

Magenta and burgundy *Ajuga reptans* 'Atropurpurea', *Allium sphaerocephalon, Buddleja davidii* 'Royal Red', *Liatris spicata, Phlox paniculata* 'Harlequin', red orach, *Viola tricolor* 'Bowles' Black'

Creams, greys and greens (used throughout to underpin colour schemes) *Achillea* 'Taygetea', artemisias in variety, *Artemisia lactiflora, Digitalis lutea,*

Phlox paniculata 'Norah Leigh', *Physostegia virginiana* 'Variegata', *Ruta graveolens* 'Jackman's Blue', *Salvia officinalis, Sisyrinchium striatum, Verbascum chaxii* 'Album'

Yellows *Achillea* 'Coronation Gold', *Anthemis tinctoria* 'E.C.Buxton', *Argyranthemum* 'Jamaica Primrose', *Iris* 'Ola Kala', *Origanum officinalis* 'Icterina', *Salvia officinalis*

OVERLEAF
LEFT *Cerise-pink flowers include irises, lupin 'The Chatelaine'. chive blossoms and a froth of* Phuopsis stylosa.

CENTRE Stachys byzantina *'Primrose Heron', yellow-green* Alchemilla mollis *and clear yellow lupins contrast with lilac-blue* Geranium pratense *'Mrs Kendall Clark' and a lilac-pink buddleja.*

RIGHT *In this section of the colour wheel, richly coloured irises are accompanied by the brighter hues of* Stachys macrantha *'Superba' and* Lavandula stoechas *subsp.* pedunculata. *The sensuous tints mark the transition from airy pastels to moodier colours.*

Golden pot
marjoram
Origanum
onites
'Aureum'

Wild
marjoram
Origanum vulgare
'Compactum'

Viola

Lavandula
stoechas
pedunculata

Thrift
Armeria

Munstead lavender
Lavandula angustifolia
'Munstead'

Lamium maculatum
'Beacon Silver'

Wild marjoram
Origanum vulgare

Bugle
Ajuga reptans

Thymus
vulgaris
'Silver Posie'

Sage
Salvia
officinalis

Viola

Pinks
Dianthus

Geranium
macrorrhizum
'Czakor'

Phuopsis
stylosa

Purple sage
Salvia officinalis
Purpurascens
Group

London
pride
Saxifraga
× *urbium*

Thymus × *citriodorus*
'Fragrantissimus'

1m
3ft

The plan and photographs on these pages show the innermost bed on the pink side of the wheel. All the central beds contain herbs such as lavender, thyme, catmint and lamium, with blue-tinted flowers or foliage, which serve as visual blenders, smoothing the transition from one colour area to another. This bed has the pale variegated thyme 'Silver Posie' at its heart.

A Classical Garden

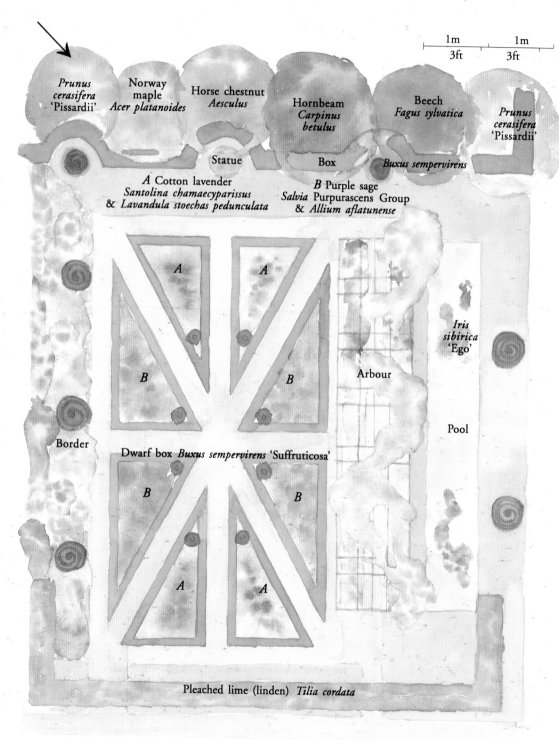

1m | **1m**
3ft | **3ft**

Prunus cerasifera 'Pissardii'

Norway maple *Acer platanoides*

Horse chestnut *Aesculus*

Hornbeam *Carpinus betulus*

Beech *Fagus sylvatica*

Prunus cerasifera 'Pissardii'

Statue

Box *Buxus sempervirens*

A Cotton lavender *Santolina chamaecyparissus* & *Lavandula stoechas pedunculata*

B Purple sage *Salvia* Purpurascens Group & *Allium aflatunense*

Iris sibirica 'Ego'

Arbour

Pool

Border

Dwarf box *Buxus sempervirens* 'Suffruticosa'

Pleached lime (linden) *Tilia cordata*

French gardens of the eighteenth century were the inspiration for this design, where herbs are used primarily for their ornamental qualities. Gardens of this period were intended to signify man's domination of nature, a philosophy that found its most complete expression in the magnificent gardens at Versailles, created by André Le Nôtre for Louis XIV.

This garden, like those on which it is modelled, relies for effect on precision geometry. The design elements include tightly clipped box hedging, topiary and a pleached *allée*, a *parterre de compartiment*, a formal pool and a precisely ordered *bosquet*. It is a garden that would fit neatly into a city plot. Its architectonic qualities would relate directly to the surrounding built environment; its 'walls' are composed of green box, pleached lime and a wooden arbour; the gravel 'floor' is broken by blocks of close-shorn grass. A mosaic of box-edged triangles (the *parterre de compartiment*) forms the focal point of the décor, which is further elaborated by a topiary-dotted herbaceous border along one side and a reflecting pool opposite. The spaces are balanced and the plantings formal.

In the parterre, herbal shrubs provide the foundation of the planting. Blocks of cotton lavender and *Lavandula stoechas* subsp. *pedunculata*

Border Mixed planting of: *Alchemilla mollis*, *Aquilegia* 'Nora Barlow', *Corylus avellana*, *Digitalis*, *Elaeagnus* × *ebbingei*, *Euphorbia amygdaloides robbiae*, *Geranium* 'Johnson's Blue', *Geranium phaeum* 'Album', *Lavandula angustifolia* 'Hidcote', *Lupinus* 'The Governor', *Nepeta* × *faassenii*, *Trachelospermum jasminoides*, *Viola* 'Princess'

Arbour *Alchemilla mollis*, *Aquilegia* 'Nora Barlow', *Geranium phaeum* 'Album', *Lavandula angustifolia* 'Hidcote', *Lavandula stoechas* subsp. *pedunculata*, *Trachelospermum jasminoides*, *Viola* 'Princess', *Wisteria sinensis*

Roses on arbour and in border *R.* 'Blanche Double de Coubert', *R.* 'Boule de Neige', *R. filipes* 'Kiftsgate', *R.* 'Frances E. Lester', *R.* 'Iceberg', *R.* 'Marchesa Boccella', *R.* 'Leverkusen', *R.* 'Sanders' White Rambler', *R.* 'Swan Lake' alternate with purple sage underplanted with *Allium aflatunense*. The silvery-grey tones and shades of purple and blue establish the colour theme for the border, with its more informal mixture of evergreen and ever-grey shrubs, roses and perennials.

In the border, the glossy dark green leaves of *Elaeagnus* × *ebbingei*, their undersides a pleasing silvery shimmer, supply an evergreen presence. Dark-flowered Hidcote lavender is ever-grey. In spring, the young foliage of catmint makes a substantial mound of grey-green, shrouded in summer by masses of powdery lilac-blue flowers. The hardy geranium 'Johnson's Blue' continues the cool tones. Slashes of wine-red come from *Euphorbia amygdaloides* var. *robbiae* and *Aquilegia* 'Nora Barlow', while the white cultivar of the mourning widow geranium, *G. phaeum* 'Album', ushers in the white roses 'Blanche Double de Coubert', 'Iceberg', 'Sanders' White Rambler', 'Swan Lake' and 'Boule de Neige'. Pale yellows complement blue and mauve, so the rose 'Leverkusen' is worked into the scheme, as is a smattering of *Alchemilla mollis*.

A substantial arbour dominates the other side of the garden; wreathed in roses, it provides a sheltered walk.

A crisply defined parterre needs to be kept in good condition. The purple sage and cotton lavender must be hard-pruned each spring; lavenders must be clipped over in the late summer and again in spring. Catmint should be shaved to the ground after flowering; it will soon make another mass of fresh foliage and a few late flowers. Roses must be pruned to keep them a good shape. There are the limes to pleach annually, topiary to keep in trim, and box edging to shear each summer. All this – plus the regular border maintenance – requires a gardener as disciplined as the garden itself. But the reward would be the feeling that you were truly in command of your domain.

An elaborate box-edged parterre terminating in a classical statue is the focal point of this manicured formal garden.

A Table of Herbs

BOTANICAL NAME COMMON NAME FAMILY	HEIGHT/ SPREAD	FORM AND HABIT/ FRUIT, FOLIAGE AND FLOWERS	SITE/ SOIL	ZONES	PROPA-GATION	REMARKS
Acanthus mollis **Bear's breeches** Acanthaceae	h1.2m/4ft s1m/3ft	Herbaceous perennial with broad glossy dark green leaves and spikes of purple and white bracts	Dry soil in sun or part-shade	7-9	Seed or division	Excellent for upright accents in the herb garden; *A. spinosus* is similar in every respect but has more deeply cut leaves and is more often used in gardens
Achillea millefolium **Yarrow, woundwort** Compositae	h45-60 cm/ 18-24in s30cm/12in	Herbaceous perennial with stiff hairy stalks supporting the umbels of small white, pink or red flowers and with leaves like long tapering feathers	Any soil in any situation	3-9	Division	Commonly recognized as a weed. 'Cerise Queen', 'Lilac Beauty' and 'White Queen' show the colour range available
Achillea ptarmica **Sneezeweed, sneezewort** Compositae	h1m/3ft s45cm/18in	Herbaceous perennial with ferny green foliage and clusters of small white button flowers	Well-drained soil in sun	3-9	Division	*A. p.* 'Boule de Neige' and 'The Pearl' are good cultivars for the herb garden. *A.* 'Moonshine' and 'Salmon Beauty' are also attractive
Aconitum napellus **Aconite, monkshood** Ranunculaceae	h1.2m/4ft s30cm/12in	Hardy herbaceous perennial with delphinium-like flower spikes in purple, blue and white	Well-drained moist soil in sun or part-shade	4-8	Seed or division	Benefits from regular replanting
Acorus calamus **Acorus, sweet flag** Acoraceae	h1m/3ft s30cm/12in	Hardy perennial herb grown for the scented foliage	Moist soil in sun or part-shade	5-9	Division	One of the old strewing herbs. It is a water's-edge plant. 'Variegatus' has creamy-yellow-streaked leaves
Aegopodium podagraria 'Variegatum' **Ground elder, goutweed** Umbelliferae	h25cm/10 in s invasive	Herbaceous perennial with cream-variegated leaves and small umbels of white flowers in summer	Poor soil in sun or part-shade	3-9	Division	Useful for groundcover in wild garden areas or clumps in gravel. Deadhead to avoid reverting seedlings
Agastache foeniculum **Anise hyssop** Labiatae	h45cm/18in s30cm/12in	Herbaceous perennial with soft grey-green foliage on erect stems bearing pale mauve flower spikes	Well-drained soil in sun or part-shade	6-8	Seed or division	Useful plant for seeding around the herb garden
A. rugosa **Korean mint**	h1m/3ft s45cm/18in	Perennial with mauve flowers over a long period. Minty leaves can be used to make tea	Any soil in sun or part-shade	7-10	Seed	
Agrostemma githago **Corncockle** Carophyllaceae	h1m/3ft s30cm/12in	Annual with pinky-purple flowers; used to be common in cornfields	Any soil in sun		Seed	
Ajuga reptans **Bugle** Labiatae	h15cm/6in s30cm/12in	Creeping perennial for groundcover. It has narrow oval mat-forming bronze-green leaves and spikes of purple or blue flowers in summer	Moist soil in sun or part-shade	4-8	Division of rooted runners	Cultivars include 'Atropurpurea' with deep purple foliage; 'Burgundy Glow', rose-pink and magenta-edged white; 'Variegata' is similar but with more restrained growth
Alchemilla mollis **Lady's mantle** Rosaceae	h45cm/18in s45cm/18in	Herbaceous perennial that makes a mound of exceptionally graceful round leaves whose crinkled edges hold the morning dew. Billowing clouds of tiny lime-green flowers in summer	Any soil in sun or part-shade	4-8	Seed or division	Self-seeds freely
Allium cepa var. *proliferum* **Tree onion, Egyptian onion** Liliaceae/Alliaceae	h45cm/18in s30cm/12in	Clump-forming evergreen perennial bearing onion bulbils at tips of leaves	Moist soil in sun	2-9	From bulbils	Use the bulbils to propagate or to make pickled onions

BOTANICAL NAME COMMON NAME FAMILY	HEIGHT/ SPREAD	FORM AND HABIT/ FRUIT, FOLIAGE AND FLOWERS	SITE/ SOIL	ZONES	PROPA-GATION	REMARKS
A. fistulosum **Welsh onion**	h45cm/18in s30cm/12in	Clump-forming evergreen perennial with white flower-heads in summer	Any soil in full sun	2-9	Seed or division	Untidy plant like giant chives; milder flavour than onions
A. schoenoprasum **Chives**	h15cm/6in s15cm/6in	Clump-forming perennial with grass-like evergreen leaves and purple flowers in late spring	Moist soil in sun or part-shade	2-9	Seed or division	Can be used as edging
A. tuberosum **Garlic chives**	h20cm/8in s15cm/6in	Clump-forming perennial with garlic-flavoured leaves and white flowers	Moist soil in sun or part-shade	3-9	Seed or division	Slow to increase
Aloysia triphylla **Lemon verbena** Verbenaceae	h1.8m/6ft s1.2m/4ft	Deciduous shrub with narrow crinkly green leaves strongly scented of citrus and small pale pink flowers	Well-drained soil in sun	8-10	Soft cuttings or seed	Can be grown outdoors, in temperate regions, against a wall with root protection. Good for training as standards to grow in pots
Althaea officinalis **Marsh mallow** Malvaceae	h1m/3ft s60cm/24in	Upright-growing perennial with pleasing soft grey-green leaves and delicate faded lavender flowers	Well-drained moist soil in sun	3-8	Seed or division	
A. rosea **Hollyhock**	h2.5m/8ft s60cm/24in	Perennial, most often grown as a biennial, that makes a towering spike with single or pompon double flowers in summer in shades from white to inky purple	Well-drained soil in sun	3-8	Seed	
Anchusa azurea **Alkanet** Boraginaceae	h1m/3ft s60cm/24in	Often short-lived perennial with gentian-blue flowers over a long period	Any soil in sun	4-7	Seed or cuttings	Can need staking
Anethum graveolens **Dill** Umbelliferae	h60cm-1m/ 2-3ft s30cm/12in	Hardy annual with soft feathery leaves	Well-drained moist soil in sun		Seed	
Angelica archangelica **Angelica** Umbelliferae	h2m/7ft s1m/3ft	Statuesque biennial flowering mid- to late summer	Any soil in sun or part-shade	4-7	Seed	One of the best structural plants for the herb garden; seeds itself freely
A. gigas	h1-1.2m/ 3-4ft s1m/3ft	Short-lived perennial. Stems and flower umbels tinged deep wine-red	Any soil in sun or part-shade	5-8	Seed	A must for colour interest
Anthemis tinctoria **Golden marguerite, dyer's camomile** Compositae	h45cm/18in s30cm/12in	Woody-stemmed perennial with grey-green foliage and bright yellow daisy flowers	Well-drained soil in sun	4-9	Division or soft cuttings	'E. C. Buxton' is a popular garden cultivar with soft butter-yellow flowers
Anthriscus cerefolium **Chervil** Umbelliferae	h60cm/24in s15cm/6in	Annual with feathery foliage	Any soil in sun or shade		Seed	Seeds itself freely
Aquilegia vulgaris **Columbine, granny's bonnet** Ranunculaceae	h1m/3ft s30cm/12in	Upright-growing herbaceous perennial with frilly glaucous foliage and nodding flowers in white and shades of pink, blue and purple	Well-drained soil in sun or part-shade	3-8	Seed or division	Flowers in early summer and looks especially pretty in combination with bluebells
Armeria maritima **Sea thrift** Plumbaginaceae	h20cm/8in s15cm/6in	Clump-forming evergreen perennial with grass-like leaves and drumsticks of pink or white flowers	Well-drained or dry soil in sun	3-7	Division or layered cuttings	Makes an unusual edging plant for knots. 'Alba' is the white-flowered cultivar

BOTANICAL NAME COMMON NAME FAMILY	HEIGHT/ SPREAD	FORM AND HABIT/ FRUIT, FOLIAGE AND FLOWERS	SITE/ SOIL	ZONES	PROPA-GATION	REMARKS
Arnica chamissonis **North American arnica** Compositae	h30cm/12in s30cm/12in	Perennial with orange daisy flowers	Well-drained soil in sun or part-shade	5-9	Seed	
Artemisia abrotanum **Southernwood, old man, lad's love** Compositae	h1m/3ft s60cm/24in	Aromatic sub-shrub with soft, finely cut grey-green foliage and sturdy upright habit	Well-drained soil in sun	5-9	Semi-ripe cuttings	A good herbal plant for vertical accent in border schemes
A. absinthium **Absinth, wormwood**	h1m/3ft s1m/3ft	Creeping perennial with narrow silver-grey leaves and silvery plumes of tiny unremarkable flowers	Well-drained soil in sun	4-9	Division	'Lambrook Silver' is the best cultivar for the garden
A. arborescens **Tree wormwood, fringed wormwood**	h1.2m/4ft s1m/3ft	Sub-shrub with finely cut, aromatic, silvery-white foliage, sprawly in habit. Can be trained up a wall for its own protection since it is tender	Well-drained soil in sun	9-10	Cuttings	The hybrid *A.* 'Powis Castle' (hardy to Z5), has the best foliage
A. dracunculus **French tarragon**	h60cm/24in s60cm/24in	Non-invasive rhizomatous perennial with shiny narrow green leaves on long stalks	Well-drained soil in sun	7-9	Division	Take care not to confuse with tasteless Russian tarragon which has duller, divided leaves
A. ludoviciana	h1.2m/4ft s60cm/24 in	Creeping perennial, taller than *A. pontica*	Well-drained soil in sun	4-9	Division	'Silver Queen' is a good named cultivar
A. pontica **Old warrior, Roman wormwood**	h30cm/12in s1m/3ft	Creeping perennial that makes clouds of silvery-white foliage	Well-drained soil in sun	5-9	Division	Makes an excellent thicket of soft foliage through which to grow other flowering herbs
Atriplex hortensis var. *rubra* **Red orach, red mountain spinach** Chenopodiaceae	h1.2m/4ft s30cm/12in	Hardy annual with tall branching stems and triangular leaves. The entire plant is coloured beetroot red	Any soil in sun or part-shade		Seed sown annually	Use like spinach, either cooked or in salad, or just let it self-seed in the garden to make curious spikes of colour
Bellis perennis **Daisy** Compositae	h15cm/6in s20cm/8in	Hardy perennial, as one knows from one's lawn! Available in named colours – white, pink and red. Good low edging plant, especially in warm climates	Any soil in sun or part-shade	3-8	Seed	
Borago officinalis **Borage** Boraginaceae	h60cm/24in s30cm/12in	Bushy annual with bristly leaves and bright blue flowers in summer	Dry to moist soil in sun	5-8	Seed	
Briza maxima **Quaking grass** Graminaceae	h45cm/18in s30cm/12in	Annual ornamental grass with nodding heads of pearly-white spikelets	Well-drained soil in sun or part-shade		Seed	
Buxus sempervirens **Common box** Buxaceae	h5m/16½ft s3m/10ft	Evergreen shrub or slow-growing small tree with small oval glossy green leaves	Well-drained soil in sun or shade	6-8	Semi-ripe cuttings	There are over 30 cultivars with varying habits and foliage forms. Can be kept pruned for hedging
B. s. 'Suffruticosa' **Dwarf box**	h60cm/24in s30cm/12in	Dwarf cultivar	Well-drained soil in sun or shade	6-8	Semi-ripe cuttings	Can be trimmed to 15cm/6in and is the hedge *sine qua non* of knot gardens and parterres
Buxus microphylla	h50cm/20in s75cm/30in	Small-growing relative of *B. sempervirens*	Well-drained soil in sun or shade	6-9	Semi-ripe cuttings	Cultivars such as 'Winter Gem' stand up well to both hot summers and cold winter temperatures, so are a good choice for harsh climates
Calamintha grandiflora **Calamint, mountain balm** Labiatae	h60cm/24in s30cm/12in	Herbaceous perennial with leaves that are mint-like in shape and taste, and pink flowers in early summer	Dry soil in sun	4-9	Semi-ripe cuttings	

BOTANICAL NAME **COMMON NAME** FAMILY	HEIGHT/ SPREAD	FORM AND HABIT/ FRUIT, FOLIAGE AND FLOWERS	SITE/ SOIL	ZONES	PROPA- GATION	REMARKS
Calendula officinalis **Marigold, pot marigold** Compositae	h30cm/12in s15cm/6in	Hardy annual with aromatic soft green leaves and abundant sunny orange and yellow daisy flowers	Dry or well-drained soil in sun		Seed	Will seed itself around, year in, year out
Caltha palustris **Marsh marigold** Ranunculaceae	h30cm/12in s45cm/18in	Hardy perennial with bright yellow flowers in spring	Moist soil in sun or shade	4-9	Seed or division	*C. p.* var. *alba* is the white variety
Carthamus tinctorius **Safflower** Compositae	h1m/3ft s60cm/24in	Annual or biennial with ragged leaves and curious thistle-like flowers with a bright orange topknot	Any well-drained soil in sun		Seed	Good for dried flower arranging
Carum carvi **Caraway** Umbelliferae	h60cm/24in s15cm/6in	Biennial with feathery foliage	Any soil in sun	3-8	Seed	
Cedronella canariensis **False balm of Gilead,** **Canary balm** Labiatae	h1m/3ft s1.2m/4ft	Tender sub-shrub with erect stems but a spreading habit, bristly dark green leaves and mauvey-pink flower spikes	Well-drained soil in sun	9-10	Seed or soft cuttings	Native to the Canaries and Madagascar, the plant has a not-unpleasant whiff of turpentine – but this plant should be banished from a low-allergen garden!
Centaurea cyanus **Cornflower** Compositae	h30cm/12in s15cm/6in	Hardy annual with felted grey stems and leaves, and bright blue, pink or white feathery flowers	Dry or well-drained soil in sun		Seed	An excellent companion for old roses. Let it find its own place in the garden
Centranthus ruber **Valerian** Valerianaceae	h1m/3ft s45cm/18in	Herbaceous perennial with glaucous foliage and upright habit, and pink or white (*C. r. albus*) flowers	Well-drained soil in sun or part-shade	4-8	Self-sows prolifically	Another good companion for old roses
Chaerophyllyum hirsutum roseum **Pink-flowered rough chervil** Umbelliferae	h60cm/24in s30cm/12in	Herbaceous pernnial with lovely feathery foliage	Any soil in sun or part-shade	5-8	Seed or division	This is the garden-worthy relative of the roadside weed rough chervil (*C. temulum*)
Chamaemelum nobile **Camomile** Compositae	h15cm/6in s30cm/12in	Hardy creeping perennial with soft wispy foliage and small daisy-like flowers	Dry soil in sun or part-shade	6-7	Seed or division	To make camomile lawns use the non-flowering cultivar 'Treneague'
Chelidonium majus **Greater celandine,** **poor man's iodine** Papaveraceae	h60cm/24in s45cm/18in	Hardy perennial with masses of pale green downy leaves on wiry stems dotted with starry yellow flowers all summer long.	Any soil in sun or part-shade	5-8	Seed or division	The stems when broken give an egg-yolk yellow sap which dabbed on insect bites is said to stop the itch. But it is poisonous so do not ingest. Prolific self-seeder
Chenopodium bonus-henricus **Good King Henry** Chenopodiaceae	h60cm/24in s30cm/12in	Hardy perennial used as a vegetable since ancient times	Any soil in sun or part-shade	4-9	Seed	
Cichorium intybus **Chicory** Compositae	h1m/3ft s30cm/12in	Hardy perennial with spikes of sky-blue flowers rising from rosettes of dandelion-like leaves	Dry soil in sun	3-7	Seed	There are also pink and white forms propagated by root cuttings
Cimicifuga racemosa **Black cohosh, bugbane** Ranunculaceae	h1.8m/6ft s60cm/24in	Hardy perennial with pure white bottlebrush flowers in summer	Any moist soil	3-8	Seed or division	

BOTANICAL NAME **COMMON NAME** FAMILY	HEIGHT/ SPREAD	FORM AND HABIT/ FRUIT, FOLIAGE AND FLOWERS	SITE/ SOIL	ZONES	PROPA- GATION	REMARKS
Consolida orientalis **Larkspur** Ranunculaceae	h1m/3ft s60cm/24in	Hardy annual of upright branching habit with feathery leaves and delphinium-like flowers in white and shades of blue, purple and pink	Dry soil in sun		Seed	
Convallaria majalis **Lily-of-the-valley** Liliaceae/ Convallariaceae	h20cm/8in s1m/3ft	Creeping herbaceous perennial to colonize in shady areas. Long flat shiny green leaves and spikes of sweetly perfumed white bells	Well-drained soil in part- or full shade	3-9	Division	*C. m.* var. *rosea* has pink flowers; 'Fortin's Giant' is a larger cultivar of the species; 'Albostriata' has yellow-streaked foliage
Coreopsis tinctoria **Coreopsis, calliopsis** Compositae	h1m/3ft s1m/3ft	Lax-growing hardy annual with thread-like foliage and bright yellow daisies with a red eye. Yields an orange dye	Well-drained or dry soil in sun		Seed	Compact selections are available
Coriandrum sativum **Coriander, cilantro** Umbelliferae	h45cm/18in s30cm/12in	Annual that looks like flat-leaved parsley but leaves have distinct tangy taste; seeds orange-flavoured	Well-drained soil in sun		Seed	
Crocus sativus **Saffron** Iridaceae	h15cm/6in s10cm/4in	Autumn-flowering crocus. Purple blooms with vivid orange stigmas. Foliage present after flowering and dies down in summer. A herb used to treat wounds and aching joints	Dry soil in sun	5-8	Division	
Cruciata laevipes **Crosswort** Rubiaceae	h45cm/18in s30cm/12in	Hardy perennial with whorls of small hairy yellowish-green leaves up the stems and bearing clusters of tiny yellow flowers in the axils during early summer	Chalky soil in sun or part-shade	5-8	Division of rooted runners	
Cuminum cyminum **Cumin** Umbelliferae	h15cm/6in s20cm/8in	Low-growing annual with feathery leaves and white flower-heads characteristic of the family	Well-drained soil in sun		Seed	
Cymbopogon citratus **Lemon grass** Gramineae	h1.5m/5ft s1m/3ft	Tender perennial useful in oriental cooking	Sun	10-11	Division	
Cynoglossum officinale **Hound's tongue** Boraginaceae	h1m/3ft s1m/3ft	Upright-growing biennial with narrow grey-green downy leaves and clusters of small faded red flowers	Dry soil in sun or part-shade	6-9	Division	A useful plant for chalky or sandy soils
Dianthus spp. and cultivars **Pinks** Caryophyllaceae	h10-60cm/ 4-24in s10-30cm/4-12in	Grey-leaved clump-forming evergreen perennial with spicily fragrant flowers in shades of pink, red and white or combinations thereof	Well-drained soil in sun	4-8	Layers or soft cuttings or seed	There are numerous species, varieties and named cultivars, some of great antiquity and all with enormous charm
D. gratianopolitanus **Cheddar pink**	h30cm/12in s30-60cm/ 12-24in	Our native pink, with a wonderful clove scent. Short-lived but easy to grow	Well-drained soil in sun	4-8	Soft cuttings or seed	
Dictamnus albus **False dittany, burning bush, gas plant** Rutaceae	h1m/3ft s60cm/24in	Aromatic divided leaves and erect spikes of white flowers in early summer	Well-drained soil in sun	3-8	Seed	
Digitalis purpurea **Foxglove** Scrophulariaceae	h1.5m/5ft s45cm/18in	Hardy biennial with tall flower spikes covered in hanging purple, pink or white bells	Well-drained soil in sun or part-shade	4-8	Seed	

BOTANICAL NAME COMMON NAME FAMILY	HEIGHT/ SPREAD	FORM AND HABIT/ FRUIT, FOLIAGE AND FLOWERS	SITE/ SOIL	ZONES	PROPA-GATION	REMARKS
D. ferruginea **Rusty foxglove**	h1.2m/4ft s60cm/24in	Narrow strap-like leaves and coppery flowers	Well-drained soil in sun or shade	5-8	Seed	
D. lanata **Woolly foxglove**	h1.2m/4ft s1m/3ft	Browny-yellow flowers and woolly foliage	Well-drained soil in sun or shade	5-8	Seed	
D. lutea **Yellow foxglove**	h1.2m/4ft s1m/3ft	Yellow-flowered foxglove	Well-drained soil in sun or shade	4-8	Seed	Makes a pleasant change from the pinky-mauve or white forms
Dryopteris filix-mas **Male fern** Dryopteridaceae	h1.2m/4ft s1m/3ft	Perennial fern with broad spreading fronds	Well-drained moist soil in shade or sun	6-8	Division	Many of the ferns have a herbal heritage and are good for those dark dank corners where few other herbal plants will thrive
Echinacea purpurea **Purple coneflower** Compositae	h1.2m/4ft s60cm/24in	Hardy herbaceous perennial with purple flowers on stiff upright stems	Well-drained soil in sun	3-8	Seed or division	A native of the prairie grasslands in the Midwest of the United States, its flowers are a striking addition to a herb scheme. 'White Swan' has white flowers tinged green
Echium vulgare **Viper's bugloss** Boraginaceae	h1.2m/4ft s1m/3ft	Biennial with hairy stems and leaves; rose-pink flowers turning to bright blue or white	Dry soil in sun	6-8	Seed	
Eruca vesicaria subsp. *sativa* **Rocket, arugula** Cruciferae	h60cm/24in s30cm/12in	Robust annual with dark green leaves and coming quickly to flower	Well-drained soil in sun		Seed	Leaves have a marked meaty savour; use sparingly in salads and in the garden - it seeds with abandon
Eryngium maritimum **Eryngo, sea holly** Umbelliferae	h30cm/12in s40cm/15in	Hardy perennial with rigid stems holding thistle flowers above ruffs of thorny-tipped leaves. The entire plant has steely blue colouring	Dry sandy soil in sun	5-8	Seed or root cuttings	A seaside plant good for dry impoverished soils. Sow seed in growing positions in autumn. Boiled roots were traditionally used as a candy
Erysimum cheiri **Wallflower** Cruciferae	h60cm/24in s45cm/18in	Biennial or short-lived perennial forming a hummock of narrow evergreen leaves topped by clusters of bright yellow, orange, red, pink or cream scented flowers	Well-drained soil in sun	7-9	Seed or semi-ripe cuttings	Double-flowered cultivars such as 'Harpur Crew' and 'Bloody Warrior' are propagated by cuttings
Eucalyptus gunnii **Eucalyptus, cider gum** Myrtaceae	h25m/80ft s12m/40ft	Makes a narrow columnar tree spreading with age. Oval grey-green leaves on juvenile trees, becoming lanceolate as the tree matures	Well-drained soil in sun	7-10	Seed	One of the hardier eucalypts. The drooping leaves make a pleasing music when stirred by the breeze. Can be pollarded to 4m/15ft
Eupatorium purpureum **Joe Pye weed** Compositae	h2.5m/8ft s1m/3ft	Herbaceous perennial of towering stature, long leaves and large rounded heads of reddish-purple flowers	Moist soil in sun	3-8	Division	One of the more architectural herbal plants to use as a focal point
Euphorbia characias subsp. *wulfenii* Euphorbiaceae	h1.2m/4ft s1m/3ft	Handsome evergreen/ever-grey foliage and long-lived yellowish-green flower spikes from earliest spring	Well-drained soil in sun	8-10	Seed	
Ficus carica **Fig** Moraceae	h5m/16½ft s5m/16½ft	A large shrub with magnificent leaves, redolent of the Mediterranean	Well-drained soil in sun	7-11		Needs a warm wall and constricted roots to produce and ripen fruit
Filipendula ulmaria **Meadowsweet** Rosaceae	h1m/3ft s60cm/24in	Hardy perennial forming clusters of finely cut leaves and sending up stiff stems topped with fluffy white flower clusters that are delicately scented	Moist or well-drained soil in sun or part-shade	3-8	Division	The leaves of the showy cultivar 'Variegata' are heavily splashed with golden yellow. 'Aurea' has pure yellow leaves

BOTANICAL NAME COMMON NAME FAMILY	HEIGHT/ SPREAD	FORM AND HABIT/ FRUIT, FOLIAGE AND FLOWERS	SITE/ SOIL	ZONES	PROPA- GATION	REMARKS
Foeniculum vulgare **Fennel** Umbelliferae	h1m/5ft s1m/3ft	Hardy perennial. The finely cut leaves have a filmy effect	Any soil in sun	4-9		At its best in early summer. The coloured foliage of 'Purpureum' (bronze fennel) is excellent with old-fashioned roses
Fragaria vesca 'Semperflorens' **Wild or alpine strawberry** Rosaceae	h30cm/12in s15cm/6in	Herbaceous clump-forming perennial with dull green leaves and tiny white flowers followed by sweet thumbnail-sized fruit	Well-drained soil in sun or part-shade	4-8	Seed or division	A good edging plant for old-fashioned potagers
Galium odoratum **Sweet woodruff** Rubiaceae	h15cm/6in s30cm/12in	Creeping herbaceous perennial with ruffs of small spiky leaves topped by clusters of tiny white stars	Well-drained moist soil in sun or part-shade	4-8	Division	Good groundcover. The dried foliage smells of new-mown hay
Gentiana lutea **Yellow gentian** Gentianaceae	h1.2m/4ft s45cm/18in	Hardy perennial. The broad soft green leaves grow in pairs up the thick stems which carry whorls of yellow spidery flowers	Deep loamy moist soil in sun	7-9	Seed	Plant in a sheltered spot. Young foliage looks like that of the false hellebore. Plants take up to three years to reach flowering size
Geranium robertianum **Herb Robert** Geraniaceae	h15cm/6in s30cm/12in	Biennial or short-lived perennial with delicate lacy leaves that are green in shade and take on a bright red blush in sun; tiny pink star-like flowers	Any soil in sun or part-shade	6-8	Self-seeds prolifically	The white-flowered form is most desirable. Both scramble through neighbouring plants and make a pretty show
G. rubescens	h60cm/24in s60cm/24in	Larger leaves than *G. robertianum* and consistently blush red	Any soil in sun or part-shade	6-10	Seed	
Hamamelis virginiana **Witch hazel** Hamamelidaceae	h4m/13ft s4m/13ft	Deciduous tree with spreading habit; fringed yellow flowers in early spring bear a fleeting scent; broad leaves colour well in autumn	Moist soil in sun or part-shade	4-9	Semi-ripe cuttings or layers	
Hedera helix **Ivy** Araliaceae	h7m/22ft s7m/22ft	Dark green five-lobed leaves	Well-drained soil in sun or shade	5-8	Soft cuttings	Familiar evergreen climber can be used as ground-cover and kept in check by hard clipping in early spring
Helianthus annuus **Sunflower** Compositae	h1.5m/5ft s1m/3ft	Towering annual with dinner-plate-sized yellow flowers	Well-drained rich soil in sun		Seed	There are dwarf hybrids like Music Box for small-garden use
Helichrysum italicum **Curry plant** Compositae	h1m/3ft s1.2m/4ft	Silvery-grey tender shrub with clusters of dirty-yellow flowers on long stems	Well-drained soil in sun	7-9	Soft cuttings	Pungently fragrant foliage is a must in the herb garden
H. splendidum	h1m/3ft s1.2m/4ft	Tender sub-shrub which makes a silvery mound and clusters of small yellow flowers	Well-drained soil in sun	8-10	Cuttings	
Helleborus foetidus **Stinking hellebore** Ranunculaceae	h45cm/18in s45cm/18in	Native perennial with deeply divided dark green leaves and clusters of pale green flowers in early spring	Any soil in shade or sun	6-9	Seed	
H. niger **Christmas rose**	h45m/18in s30cm/12in	Herbaceous perennial with leathery palmate leaves and clusters of white flowers in winter	Well-drained soil in sun or part-shade	4-7	Seed or division	
Hesperis matronalis **Sweet rocket** Cruciferae	h1.2m/4ft s1m/3ft	Herbaceous perennial with dull foliage; clusters of sweetly fragrant white or purple flowers in early summer	Well-drained soil in sun or part-shade	4-8	Seed or division	Use at the back of the border to hide its lanky growth

BOTANICAL NAME / COMMON NAME / FAMILY	HEIGHT/ SPREAD	FORM AND HABIT/ FRUIT, FOLIAGE AND FLOWERS	SITE/ SOIL	ZONES	PROPA-GATION	REMARKS
Hippophaë rhamnoides **Sea buckthorn, sallow thorn** Elaeagnaceae	h3m/10ft s1.5m/5ft	Deciduous suckering shrub forming thickets. Lanceo-late leaves are silvery grey with brown reverse; the tiny green flowers are followed by wonderful copper berries (if both male and female plants grown)	Dry soil in sun	4-8	Suckers or semi-ripe cuttings	This seaside-loving plant thrives in sandy soil, but inlanders should try to accommodate it for the splendid colouring. Can be pruned into a small tree
Humulus lupulus **Hop** Cannabidaceae	h5m/16½ft s2m/7ft	Perennial climber with broad palmate leaves. Male plants have panicles of papery soft green 'flowers'; female have short cone-like spikes	Well-drained soil in sun	6-9	Division	Female plant is usually grown
H. l. 'Aureus' **Golden hop**	h5m/16½ft s2m/7ft	Bright apple-green foliage; lacks the showy hop-heads of its green-leaved cousin	Well-drained soil in sun	6-9	Division	
Hypericum patulum **St John's wort** Guttiferae	h1m/3ft s1m/3ft	Deciduous low-growing spreading shrub with bright yellow flowers	Well-drained soil in sun	6-8	Soft cuttings	
Hyssopus officinalis **Hyssop** Labiatae	h60cm/24in s30cm/12in	Shrubby perennial that has narrow soft green leaves topped by spikes of pale lavender-blue flowers. There are white- and pink-flowered forms	Well-drained soil in sun	6-9	Seed or soft cuttings	To make a lovely low knot-garden hedge clip it hard back in early spring before flowering, or afterwards if soft colour is more important than hard lines
Inula helenium **Elecampane** Compositae	h1.5m/5ft s1m/3ft	Upright-growing herbaceous perennial with many bright yellow flowers in summer	Well-drained or dry soil in sun	5-8	Seed or Division	A rugged individual; untidy but useful for emphasis in borders
Iris 'Florentina' **Florentine iris, orris** Iridaceae	h1m/3ft s1m/3ft	Perennial rhizome with pale grey-green sword-like leaves and violet-scented flowers of subtle shimmery silver-blue	Well-drained soil in sun or part-shade	6-8	Division	The dried root is a source of orris powder used in perfumery and the making of potpourri (the root of *I. pallida* is another)
I. foetidissima **Gladwyn, stinking iris**	h45cm/18in s60cm/24in	Creeping rhizomatous evergreen with glossy green leaf blades and insignificant flowers, followed by large seed-pods that burst open to reveal orange bead-like seeds	Any soil in sun	5-8	Division	The crushed leaves smell of roast beef, but it is the seed capsules that excite flower arrangers. 'Citrina' has more attractive flowers; 'Variegata' is cheerful
I. pseudacorus **Yellow flag**	h1m/3ft s45cm/18in	Rhizomatous perennial with bright yellow flowers veined with purple	Wet soil at water's edge	5-8	Division	Also known as fleur-de-lys, the French royal crest. The young foliage of 'Variegata' is yellow edged with green, turning pale green with age
I. versicolor **Blue flag, poison flag**	h60cm/24in s60cm/24in	Rhizomatous perennial with blue flowers that open to be quite flat and lax; soft foliage	Wet soil at water's edge	4-8	Division	A herbal plant of native North Americans; 'Kermesina' has reddish-purple flowers
Isatis tinctoria **Woad** Cruciferae	h1m/3ft s60cm/24in	Biennial with glaucous leaves and small yellow flowers, followed by sprays of black seedheads	Dry soil in sun	6-8	Seed	Better looking than it sounds; the seedheads have a pleasing glitter to them
Jasminum officinale **Jasmine, poet's jasmine** Oleaceae	h5m/16½ft s5m/16½ft	Vigorous shrubby climber with star-like white flowers set amid glossy dark green foliage; highly scented	Well-drained soil in full sun	8-10	Soft cuttings	
Juniperus communis **Juniper** Cupressaceae	h1.5m/5ft s1.5m/5ft	Evergreen conifer; black berries	Well-drained soil in sun	3-7	Semi-ripe cuttings	Useful for foundation planting in herb borders. The dried berries are used for flavouring
Lamium maculatum **Variegated dead nettle** Labiatae	h15cm/6in s spreading	Spreading perennial with colours ranging from white to purple	Any soil in sun or shade	4-8	Division	

BOTANICAL NAME **COMMON NAME** FAMILY	HEIGHT/ SPREAD	FORM AND HABIT/ FRUIT, FOLIAGE AND FLOWERS	SITE/ SOIL	ZONES	PROPA- GATION	REMARKS
L. × galeobdolon **Yellow archangel**	h15cm/6in s invasive	Yellow flowers	Any soil in sun or shade	4-9	Division	
Laurus nobilis **Bay** Lauraceae	h5m/16½ft s3m/10ft	Evergreen shrub with glossy ovate leaves	Well-drained soil in sun or part-shade	8-10	Cuttings	Can be left to grow to its natural size or kept clipped for formal topiary features. 'Aurea' is the yellow-leaved cultivar
Lavandula angustifolia **Lavender, English lavender** Labiatae	h1.2m/4ft s1.2m/4ft	Grey-leaved evergreen shrub with spikes of purple flowers; every part of the plant is scented	Well-drained soil in sun	5-8	Seed or soft cuttings	There are numerous cultivars of varying heights and colours, e.g. 'Hidcote', 'Loddon Pink' and 'Munstead'. Also try *L. × intermedia* 'Grappenhall' and the hybrid 'Sawyers'
L. stoechas **French lavender, Spanish lavender**	h60/24in 260cm/24in	Neat mound-forming shrub with soft grey foliage and flowers held in tight buds topped with little papery bracts, like small purple pineapples	Well-drained soil in sun	8-9	Semi-ripe cuttings	Not hardy, so give some shelter. *L. s.* subsp. *pedunculata* is showier with more pronounced bracts atop the flower-heads
Levisticum officinale **Lovage** Umbelliferae	h1.5m/5ft s1m/3ft	Substantial perennial with bold glossy foliage and large flower umbels in late summer	Moist soil in sun or part- shade	4-8	Seed	Good architectural plant for the herb border
Liatris spicata **Gay feather, blazing star** Compositae	h60cm/24in s30cm/12in	Herbaceous perennial with upright stems covered in narrow grass-like leaves and bearing bubblegum-pink flower spikes	Well-drained moist soil in sun	3-8	Seed or division	'Alba' is the white-flowered cultivar
Linaria purpurea **Toadflax** Scrophulariaceae	h1m/3ft s45cm/18in	Narrow greyish leaves up a flower spike bearing snap-dragon-like flowers ranging from white to purple	Well-drained soil in sun	5-8	Seed	Seeds itself pleasantly, not overbearingly
Linum perenne **Perennial flax** Linaceae	h45cm/18in s15cm/6in	Hardy perennial with wiry stems covered in short narrow leaves and bearing clear cobalt-blue flowers at the tips	Well-drained soil in sun	5-8	Seed	Extremely graceful when a breeze wafts the stems back and forth
Lobelia cardinalis **Cardinal flower** Campanulaceae	h1m/3ft s30cm/12in	Hardy herbaceous perennial with erect flower stems, green foliage and scarlet flower spikes in summer	Moist soil in sun or part- shade	3-8	Seed or division	Valuable for its red colouring but must have a damp site to perform well
L. siphilitica **Great or blue lobelia**	h1.2m/4ft s30cm/12in	Hardy perennial with pale green leaves along the upright stem and bright blue flowers in the leaf axils	Well-drained soil in sun or part-shade	4-8	Seed or division	Used by the North American Iroquois to treat venereal disease, and by other tribes as an aphro-disiac. Brings a blue accent to the herb garden
Lysimachia nummularia 'Aurea' **Golden creeping Jenny** Primulaceae	h5cm/2in	Ground-hugging creeper that covers the soil with bright yellow-green foliage and yellow flowers	Moist soil in shade	5-8	Division	This will brighten up dank corners
Marrubium vulgare **Horehound** Labiatae	h60cm/24in s1m/3ft	Shrubby perennial with small round pale grey felted leaves and whorls of pale lilac flowers in summer	Well-drained soil in sun	3-8	Seed or division	The flowers are not particularly exciting, so clip over regularly to stop it looking bedraggled
Melianthus major Melianthaceae	h1.8m/6ft s1.8m/6ft	A tender shrub, often cut down by frost but will sprout again from the base; beautiful grey-green deeply serrated foliage	Any soil in sun	9-10	Seed or division	The leaves are pungently scented of burnt chocolate
Melissa officinalis **Lemon balm** Labiatae	h1m/3ft s1m/3ft	Herbaceous perennial with bristly leaves and vigorous spreading habit; strongly scented of citrus	Well-drained soil in sun or part-shade	6-8	Seed or division	'All Gold' has pure yellow leaves that scorch in sun; 'Aurea' is strongly marked with flashes of yellow on green

BOTANICAL NAME **COMMON NAME** FAMILY	HEIGHT/ SPREAD	FORM AND HABIT/ FRUIT, FOLIAGE AND FLOWERS	SITE/ SOIL	ZONES	PROPA- GATION	REMARKS
Mentha **Mint** Labiatae	h45cm/18in s invasive	Familiar spreading perennial	Moist soil in sun or shade	6-8	Division	Mint is best given its own corner to dominate
M. × gracilis 'Variegata' **Ginger mint, golden ginger mint**	h45cm/18in s invasive	Creeping perennial	Moist soil in sun or shade	4-8	Division	Golden variegation and dark stems make this very attractive, but beware: extremely invasive
M. longifolia **Horse mint**	h60cm/24in s invasive	Fast-spreading perennial with grey felted stems and foliage	Dry to moist soil in sun or shade	6-8	Division	Not a culinary mint: has a hint of mothballs in a cupboard about it
M. × piperita **Peppermint**	h45cm/18in s invasive	Creeping perennial with bright green, highly flavoured foliage	Moist soil in sun or shade	4-8	Division	
M. × piperita citrata **Eau de cologne mint**	h45cm/18in s invasive	Purple-tinted leaves and stems on creeping perennial	Moist soil in sun or shade	4-8	Division	
M. pulegium **Pennyroyal**	h30cm/12in s invasive	Spreading perennial with strong peppermint scent	Moist soil in shade	5-9	Division	
M. requienii **Corsican mint**	h5mm/¼in s45cm/18in	Mat-forming, tiny-leaved creeping perennial	Moist soil in sun or shade	6-9	Division	Good for growing in and along paths
M. × rotundifolia **Apple mint, round-leaved mint**	h60cm/24in s invasive	Velvety large round grey-leaved perennial	Moist soil in sun or shade	5-8	Division	
M. spicata **Spearmint**	h45cm/18in s invasive	Creeping perennial with pale green foliage	Moist soil in sun or shade	4-8	Division	
M. s. 'Crispa' **Curly mint**	h30cm/12in s invasive	Spreading perennial with cut and curly leaf edges	Moist soil in sun or shade	4-8	Division	
M. suaveolens 'Variegata' **Pineapple mint**	h30cm/12in s invasive	Creeping perennial with foliage variegated white and cream	Moist soil in shade	6-8	Division	
M. × villosa f. *alopecuroïdes* **Bowles' mint**	h1m/3ft s invasive	Hardy perennial with soft green hairy leaves	Moist soil in sun or light shade	4-9	Division	
Milium effusum 'Aureum' **Bowles' golden grass** Gramineae	h40cm/15in s30cm/12in	Non-invasive clumps of soft yellow grass with bead-like flowers in early summer	Any soil in part-shade	5-8	Seed or division	
Monarda didyma **Bergamot, bee balm, Oswego tea** Labiatae	h1m/3ft s60cm/24in	Hardy herbaceous perennial with stiff upright habit and bright red flower-heads	Moist soil in sun	4-8	Division	This citrus-scented plant can be disfigured by mildew. Good coloured hybrids available include 'Cambridge Scarlet' and 'Croftway Pink'
Myrrhis odorata **Sweet cicely** Umbelliferae	h1.2m/4ft s1m/3ft	Easy upright-growing perennial with bright green ferny foliage and umbels of white flowers	Well-drained soil in sun or part-shade	4-8	Seed or division	Makes a stunning clump of graceful foliage
Myrtus communis **Myrtle** Myrtaceae	h3m/10ft s1.5m/5ft	Evergreen shrub with small shiny green leaves and small creamy white flowers	Well-drained soil in sun	8-10	Semi-ripe cuttings	Hardy to Z8 with winter protection or against a wall; otherwise Z9. Scented in all its parts

BOTANICAL NAME COMMON NAME FAMILY	HEIGHT/ SPREAD	FORM AND HABIT/ FRUIT, FOLIAGE AND FLOWERS	SITE/ SOIL	ZONE	PROPA-GATION	REMARKS
Nepeta × faassenii **Catmint** Labiatae	h30cm/12in s60cm/24in	Small soft grey leaves and pale lavender flower spikes on a lax herbaceous perennial	Well-drained soil in sun	4-8		Makes a good soft edging plant. 'Six Hills Giant' is a larger version spreading to 1.2m/4ft
N. govaniana	h1m/3ft s60cm/24in	Hardy perennial with pointed leaves and long-tubed flowers of a clear light yellow	Moist soil in shade or part-shade	5-8	Seed, soft cuttings or division	
Nicotiana rustica **Tobacco** Solanaceae	h1.5m/5ft s1m/3ft	Perennial grown as a half-hardy annual with broad flat leaves and spikes of tubular pink flowers	Well-drained soil in sun	8-10	Seed	'Statuesque' best describes this tobacco plant
N. sylvestris	h1.5m/5ft s1m/3ft	Perennial grown as a half-hardy annual. Long narrow pure white flowers that are deliciously scented in the evening	Well-drained soil in sun	8-10	Seed	
Nigella damascena **Love-in-a-mist** Ranunculaceae	h45cm/18in s10cm/4in	Upright-growing hardy annual with feathery foliage and blue, white or pink flowers like a ballerina's tutu	Well-drained soil in sun		Seed	Let this charming flower seed itself to blur the edges of herbaceous plantings
N. hispanica	h45cm/18in s10cm/4in	Larger black-centred flowers	Well-drained soil in sun		Seed	
Nymphaea alba **Water lily** Nymphaeaceae	s3m/10ft	Broad green dishes float on the water with star-like white flowers	Still water in sun or part-shade	5-9	Division	The classic perennial for pools and still-water features
Ocimum basilicum **Sweet basil** Labiatae	h30cm/12in s30cm/12in	Tender bushy annual with broad green highly scented leaves	Moist soil in full sun		Seed	Look also for frilly-leaved 'Green Ruffles'
O. b. var. *citriodorum* **Lemon basil**	h30cm/12in s30cm/12in	Tender annual with narrow leaves	Moist soil in full sun		Seed	There are also liquorice- and cinnamon-flavoured basils
O. b. var. *minimum* **Bush basil**	h15cm/6in s10cm/4in	Small leaves and compact rounded habit	Moist soil in full sun		Seed	Excellent for annual edging in a potager
O. b. var. *purpurascens* **Purple basil**	h30cm/12in s30cm/12in	Tender annual with broad purple leaves	Moist soil in full sun		Seed	Look also for large-leaved 'Purple Opal' and frilly-leaved 'Purple Ruffles'
O. tenuiflorum **Holy basil**	h30cm/12in s30cm/12in	Greenish-purple leaves with serrated edges	Moist soil in full sun		Seed	
Oenothera biennis **Evening primrose** Onagraceae	h1.2m/4ft s45cm/18in	Upright-growing hardy biennial with bright yellow trumpet-shaped flowers that open at night on red-tinted stalks	Well-drained or dry soil in sun	6-8	Seed	
O. stricta 'Sulphurea'	h1m/3ft s45cm/18in	More refined in colour and stature	Well-drained or dry soil in sun	5-8	Seed	
Onopordum acanthium **Cotton thistle** Compositae	h2.5m/8ft s1.2m/4ft	Hardy biennial which makes broad rosettes of grey felt leaves in the first year and a towering flower stem the second	Any soil in sun	5-9	Self-seeds freely	Also known as the Scotch thistle, this is a real show stopper in the border, so weed out seedlings judiciously

BOTANICAL NAME / COMMON NAME / FAMILY	HEIGHT/ SPREAD	FORM AND HABIT/ FRUIT, FOLIAGE AND FLOWERS	SITE/ SOIL	ZONES	PROPA- GATION	REMARKS
Origanum onites **Pot marjoram** Labiatae	h45cm/18cm s30cm/12in	Tender perennial with grey-green leaves and white or pink flowers	Dry soil in full sun	8-9	Seed	In cold climates best treated as an annual or pot-grown
O. vulgare **Oregano, wild marjoram**	h45cm/18in s30cm/12in	Hardy shrubby perennial with mauve flowers in early summer	Dry soil in sun or part-shade	6-9	Division	Varieties worth having include 'Compactum', 'Gold Tip', 'Aureum Crispum' and 'Golden Shine'
O. v. 'Aureum' **Golden marjoram**	h45cm/18cm s30cm/12in	The yellow-leaved cultivar of wild oregano	Dry soil in full sun	6-9	Seed	
O. v. hirtum **Greek oregano**	h60cm/24in s45cm/18in	Strongest flavour for culinary purposes	Dry soil in full sun	9	Seed	
Paeonia officinalis **Peony** Paeoniaceae	h1m/3ft s1m/3ft	Hardy herbaceous perennial with strong foliage that colours well in autumn	Well-drained soil in sun or part-shade	4-7	Division	*P. o.* 'Rubra Plena' has wine-red pompon flowers
Papaver orientale **Oriental poppy** Papaveraceae	h1m/3ft s1m/3ft	Perennial with rosettes of prickly leaves and large single white flowers from cardinal red through wine-stain purple to white	Well-drained soil in sun	3-7	Root cuttings or division	Hard to rival for a showy splash of colour in early summer. Use at the back of the border, since there is not much to look at once the flowers are over
P. rupifragum 'Flore Pleno'	h45cm/18in s30cm/12in	Perennial with narrow grey-green leaves and delicate semi-double flowers with petals like pale orange silk	Well-drained soil in sun	8-9	Seed or root cuttings	A lovely little plant to dot along the edge of the border or scatter among blue- and mauve-flowered plantings
P. somniferum **Opium poppy**	h60cm/24in s30cm/12in	Hardy annual with grey ruffled leaves and large fully double frilly flowers in shades of red, pink, purple or white	Any soil in sun		Self-seeds prolifically	An inhabitant of a physic garden since the Crusades
Passiflora caerulea **Passion flower** Passifloraceae	h5m/16½ft s3m/10ft	Vigorous straggly climber with large vivid flowers followed by egg-shaped fruits that ripen bright orange	Well-drained soil in sun or part-shade	7-10	Semi-ripe cuttings	Fast-growing but untidy
Pelargonium species and cultivars **Scented geraniums, scented pelargoniums** Geraniaceae	h15-30cm/ 6-12in s75cm/30in or more	Tender shrubby evergreens; vary widely in foliage shape and colour and showiness of flowers	Well-drained soil in sun	9-10	Soft cuttings	Treat as pot plants in all but the warmest climates. *P. graveolens, P. crispum* 'Variegatum', *P. × fragrans* and *P.* 'Lady Plymouth' are just a few for collection
Pentaglottis sempervirens (syn. *Anchusa sempervirens*) **Wood alkanet** Boraginaceae	h60cm/24in s60cm/24in	Blue flowers over a long period; rather coarse foliage	Any soil in sun or shade	4-8	Seed	
Perilla frutescens var. *crispa* **Shiso, Japanese perilla, Vietnamese herb** Labiatae	h45cm/18in s30cm/12in	Half-hardy annual with broad crinkly aromatic green or purple leaves	Well-drained soil in sun		Seed sown in spring	Easy to grow, the leaves look and taste mildly like basil. Use the red-leaved varieties as dot plants in bedding schemes or formal herbal plantings
Perovskia atriplicifolia **Russian sage** Labiatae	h1.2m/4ft s45cm/18in	Spikes of lavender-blue flowers on grey-white stems, lovely in winter	Well-drained soil in sun	5-9	Seed or soft cuttings	
Persicaria bistorta (syn. *Polygonum bistorta*) **Bistort, snakeroot** Polygonaceae	h1m/3ft s1.2m/4ft	Clump-forming rhizomatous perennial with long oval leaves and spikes of rosy-pink flowers in early summer	Well-drained soil in sun or shade	3-9	Division	'Superba' with soft pink flowers is the garden cultivar to look for. Can be invasive

BOTANICAL NAME COMMON NAME FAMILY	HEIGHT/ SPREAD	FORM AND HABIT/ FRUIT, FOLIAGE AND FLOWERS	SITE/ SOIL	ZONES	PROPA- GATION	REMARKS
Petroselinum crispum **Moss-curled parsley** Umbelliferae	h30cm/12in s30cm/12in	Familiar biennial leaf herb	Moist soil in sun or part-shade	6-8	Seed	Good for edging. Best grown as an annual in zones colder than 6
P. c. neapolitanum **Flat-leaved parsley, Italian parsley**	h45cm/18in s30cm/12in	Upright-growing stiff stems and masses of bright green flat leaves	Moist soil in sun or part-shade	6-8	Seed	Germinates more quickly than moss-curled parsley. Also known as French parsley
Phlomis fruticosa **Jerusalem sage** Labiatae	h1.2m/4ft s1.2m/4ft	Grey woolly-leaved shrub with rounded form and erect flowering stems bearing whorls of egg-yolk yellow flowers in early summer	Dry soil in sun	7-9	Soft cuttings or seed	Prune after flowering to prevent legginess
P. italica	h75cm/30in s1m/3ft	Lilac-pink flowers, grey leaves	Dry soil in sun	9-10	Soft cuttings	
P. russeliana	h1.2m/4ft s1m/3ft	Evergreen perennial with broad heart-shaped leaves and whorls of yellow flowers in the leaf axils up the tall erect stems	Any soil in sun or part-shade	4-8	Seed or division	Wonderful substantial groundcover; the dried seedheads are a bonus for flower arranging
Phuopsis stylosa Rubiaceae	h30cm/12in s60cm/24in	Front of border perennial with pink flowers over a long period; its shiny green foliage is aromatic	Any soil in sun	5-8	Division	'Purpurea' has deeper-coloured flowers
Phyllostachys **Bamboo** Gramineae/Bambusoideae	h2.5-9m/ 8-30ft s2m/7ft	One of the least invasive genus of bamboos, with a wide variety of leaf and stem colour	Any soil	6-10	Division	
Physalis alkekengi **Cape gooseberry, Chinese lantern** Solanaceae	h60cm/24in s60cm/24in	Herbaceous perennial with unkempt appearance; broad leaves and straggly stems. Brilliant orange lantern-shaped seed pods in autumn	Well-drained soil in sun or part-shade	6-8	Division	A plant or two dotted at the front of the border where the low autumn light can catch the seed pods is most effective
Pimpinella anisum **Anise** Umbelliferae	h60cm/24in s30cm/12in	Annual with lace-like foliage and flower-heads	Dry soil in shade		Seed	
P. saxifraga **Burnet saxifrage** Umbelliferae	h1m/3ft s30cm/12in	Short-lived hardy herbaceous perennial with finely cut chervil-like foliage and delicate lacy white flowers	Dry soil in sun or part-shade	4-8	Seed	Ancient herb now most often seen in hedge banks. The flowers have a wonderful frothy effect
Plantago major **Plantain, rat's-tail plantain** Plantaginaceae	h25-35cm/ 10-14in s20-35cm/ 8-10in	Herbaceous perennial. Broad flat-leaved rosettes frame the flower spikes that look just like a rat's tail	Any soil and any aspect	3-7	Seed	Commonly regarded as a lawn-spoiling weed. The bloody plantain 'Rubrifolia' with large ovate red-tinged leaves and rose plantain *P. m.* 'Rosularis', with its rose-like green flowers are more garden-worthy
Polemonium caeruleum **Jacob's ladder** Polemoniaceae	h60cm/24in s30cm/12in	Erect-growing perennial with soft green, ladder-like leaves and blue flower spikes	Well-drained rich soil in sun or part-shade	4-8	Self-sown seed or division	Good for early summer flowers; several named cultivars in shades of blue, mauve, pink and white
P. reptans	h30cm/12in s25cm/10in	Low-growing, with soft green pinnate leaves and clusters of bright blue flowers	Well-drained rich soil in sun or part-shade	4-8	Self-sown seed or division	Also worth growing and good for early summer flowers
Portulaca oleracea **Purslane** Portulacaceae	h15cm/6in h30cm/12in	Succulent green-leaved tender annual	Dry soil in sun		Seed	Useful groundcover in parched areas of the garden. Leaves used in salads

BOTANICAL NAME COMMON NAME FAMILY	HEIGHT/ SPREAD	FORM AND HABIT/ FRUIT, FOLIAGE AND FLOWERS	SITE/ SOIL	ZONES	PROPA-GATION	REMARKS
Primula elatior **Oxlip** Primulaceae	h30cm/12in s15cm/6in	Herbaceous spring-flowering perennial with erect stalks rising from a rosette of crinkly green leaves and bearing umbels of yellow flowers	Moist soil in part-shade	5-7	Seed or division	Similar in habit to a cowslip, but with much more delicate flowers
P. veris **Cowslip**	h30cm/12in s15cm/6in	Herbaceous perennial making flat rosettes of leaves with upright stalks of yellow flower umbels in spring	Moist or well-drained soil in sun or part-shade	5-7		A meadow herb that will naturalize in lawns or among bulbs and early spring flowers
P. vulgaris **Primrose, English primrose**	h15cm/6in s15cm/6in	Clump-forming perennial with soft crinkled leaves and small yellow flowers	Moist soil in sun or part-shade	6-7	Self-sown seed or division	
Pulmonaria officinalis **Lungwort** Boraginaceae	h30cm/12in s30cm/12in	Clump-forming hardy perennial , with several named varieties and cultivars. Long oval leaves blotched silvery-white and having pink, blue or white flowers in spring	Well-drained or moist soil in part- or full shade	4-8	Division	Good for interplanting with snowdrops, hellebores and other early flowers. 'Sissinghurst White' is a favourite; also *P.* 'Blue Ensign', 'Mournful Purple' and 'David Ward'
P. angustifolia	h30cm/12in s30cm/12in	Has plain dark green leaves and flowers that turn from pink to blue with age	Well-drained or moist soil in part- or full shade	3-8	Division	
P. longifolia	h30cm/12in s30cm/12in	The leaves are long and narrow, spotted with white, and the flowers are a good bright blue	Well-drained or moist soil in part- or full shade	4-8	Division	
P. saccharata	h30cm/12in s30cm/12in	The leaves can be larger than *P. officinalis*. The flowers are a rich violet-blue	Moist soil in part- or full shade	3-8	Division	
Pulsatilla vulgaris rubra **Pasque flower** Ranunculaceae	h30cm/12in s30cm/12in	Perennial with finely cut soft foliage and velvety purple flowers	Well-drained soil in sun	6-7	Seed or division	
Ranunculus acris 'Flore Pleno' **Double buttercup** Ranunculaceae	h1m/3ft s30cm/12in	Well-behaved clump-forming perennial	Any fairly moist soil in sun or part-shade	4-8	Division	
Reseda odorata **Mignonette** Resedaceae	h30cm/12in s30cm/12in	Annual with creamy-brown fragrant flowers	Well-drained soil in sun		Seed	
Rheum × hybridum **Rhubarb** Polygonaceae	h1.2m/4ft s1.2m/4ft	Herbaceous perennial with large fan-shaped leaves and edible stalks. Creamy-coloured flower spike sets red-tinted seed	Well-drained or moist soil in sun or part-shade	3-7	Seed or division	This is the species common to vegetable gardens and used for culinary purposes
R. palmatum **Turkey rhubarb**	h2m/7ft s1.2m/4ft	Similar in growth and habit to familiar rhubarb but the leaves have narrower stems and deeply toothed edges; the flower is also more showy	Well-drained rich soil in sun or part-shade	4-7	Division	'Hadspen Crimson' and 'Bowles' Crimson' have good red colouring in leaf and stem
Ribes odoratum **Buffalo currant** Grossulariaceae	h2.5m/8ft s2m/7ft	Deciduous shrub with pale green toothed leaves and spicily scented yellow flowers, followed by dark purple berries	Any soil in sun or part-shade	5-8	Seed or semi-ripe cuttings	Untidy, lanky habit of growth but cutting the branches for indoors will help keep the shrub in shape

BOTANICAL NAME / COMMON NAME / FAMILY	HEIGHT/ SPREAD	FORM AND HABIT/ FRUIT, FOLIAGE AND FLOWERS	SITE/ SOIL	ZONES	PROPA- GATION	REMARKS
Rosa spp. and cultivars **Rose** Rosaceae	h1.2-2m/4-7ft s1-1.4m/3-5ft					The most familiar of flowering shrubs. There are hundreds to choose from but for herb garden purposes choose the old shrub roses or species
R. canina **Dog rose, briar rose**	h5m/16½ft s3m/10ft	Scrambling rose with long arching stems and simple single pink flowers followed by tiny orange hips	Any soil in sun	3-8	Soft cuttings	The common wild rose found in hedgerows can be translated to the garden hedge. Pruned it will stay within bounds and provide plenty of hips
R. × damascena 'Professeur Emile Perrot'	h1.8m/6ft s1.5m/5ft	Spindly shrub with soft green leaves and small loosely double pink flowers in summer	Well-drained soil in sun	4-8	Soft cuttings	Produces attar of roses for the perfume trade. Often (wrongly) called *R. × d.* 'Tringintipetala', the Kanzalik rose
R. eglanteria **Sweetbriar rose, eglantine**	h1.8m/6ft s1.5m/5ft	Prickly upright-growing shrub with small leathery leaves and pale pink flowers followed by small red hips	Well-drained soil in sun	4-8	Soft cuttings	On humid days or following rain a breeze will waft ripe-apple scent from the foliage. The hybrid 'Magnifica' lives up to its name with a curtain of flowers in early summer, a neat habit for hedging and plenty of scent
R. gallica officinalis **The apothecary's rose**	h1m/3ft s1m/3ft	Upright-growing shrub with leathery dull green leaves and abundant highly scented single deep pink flowers in summer followed by bright red hips	Well-drained enriched soil in sun	4-8	Soft cuttings	This is *the* rose of the herb garden: the petals can be used to flavour foods, to make the highly effica- cious rose vinegar and dried for potpourri
R. 'Complicata'	h5-10m/ 16½-33ft s3m/10ft	A similar but larger hybrid of the apothecary's rose	Any soil in sun	4-9	Soft cuttings	
R. g. 'Versicolor' **Rosa Mundi**		A cultivar of the apothecary's rose but with hand- somely variegated flowers	Any soil in sun	4-8	Soft cuttings	
R. primula **The incense rose**	h2m/7ft s1.5m/5ft	Sturdy rose covered in tiny butter-yellow flowers from spring to early summer	Any soil in sun	5-8	Semi-ripe or hardwood cuttings	
R. rugosa **Turkestan rose, Japanese rose**	h1.8m/6ft s1.5m/5ft	Rugged dense thorny bush with upright habit, leathery crinkled leaves and large single pink flowers followed by large red hips	Well-drained soil in sun	2-9	Soft cuttings or seed	An exceedingly robust rose from Japan, it is one of the few roses that will grow near the sea and survive temperature extremes. 'Scabrosa' has especially large flowers and hips and a strong spicy scent
Rosmarinus officinalis **Rosemary** Labiatae	h1.2m/4ft s1m/3ft	Loose spreading evergreen shrub with narrow highly fragrant glossy leaves and pale to dark blue flowers	Well-drained soil in sun	7-9	Semi-ripe cuttings	Often used for hedging, but can be short-lived
R.o. var. *albiflorus* **White-flowered rosemary**	h1.2m/4ft s1m/3ft	As *R. officinalis*, but with white flowers	Well-drained soil in sun	7-9	Semi-ripe cuttings	Suitable for training against a wall
R. o. 'Aureus' **Gilded rosemary**	h60cm/24in s80cm/32in	Rarer and somewhat more tender rosemary with gold- splashed leaves	Well-drained soil in sun	8-10	Semi-ripe cuttings	
R.o. 'Miss Jessopp's Upright' **Upright rosemary**	h1.5m/5ft s1.2m/4ft	Upright-growing cultivar	Well-drained soil in sun	7-9	Semi-ripe cuttings	Suitable for training against a wall
R.o. Prostratus Group **Creeping rosemary**	h50cm/20in s1.2m/3½ft	As *R. officinalis*	Well-drained soil in sun	8-9	Semi-ripe cuttings	Prostrate-growing form suitable for raised beds and containers. Especially tender
Rumex acetosa **Garden sorrel** Polygonaceae	h60cm/24in s45cm/18in	Perennial with broad green leaves appearing early summer and red-tinged flower spikes	Well-drained soil in sun or part-shade	3-7	Division	Will seed itself around the garden

BOTANICAL NAME COMMON NAME FAMILY	HEIGHT/ SPREAD	FORM AND HABIT/ FRUIT, FOLIAGE AND FLOWERS	SITE/ SOIL	ZONES	PROPA-GATION	REMARKS
R. sanguineus var. *sanguineus* **Red-veined dock**	h1m/3ft s60cm/24in	Wine-red veins and stems to the green leaves	Dry soil in sun	6-7	Seed or division	This ornamental member of the tribe will seed itself around the garden
R. scutatus **Buckler-leaved sorrel, French sorrel**	h7.5cm/3in s10cm/4in	Ground-hugging rosette-forming perennial 'weed'; the leaves are spade-shaped	Moist soil in sun or part-shade	6-7	Seed or division	Common in waste ground. The leaves are astringently juicy and a good addition to salads
Ruta graveolens **Rue** Rutaceae	h1m/3ft s65cm/2ft	Upright-growing shrub with glaucous lacy leaves and chartreuse-yellow flowers in summer	Well-drained soil in sun	5-8	Soft cuttings	A good companion for purple and mauve roses and in silver or grey planting schemes. 'Jackman's Blue' has the best colour; 'Variegata' is splashed with cream
Salvia officinalis **Sage** Labiatae	h75cm/30in s75cm/30in	Grey-leaved low-spreading shrub with soft blue flowers in early summer	Well-drained soil in sun	6-9	Seed or soft cuttings	To keep plant shapely cut off faded flower stems and clip in early spring to remove dead stems and straggly growth
S.o. 'Albiflora' **White-flowered sage**	h75cm/30in s75cm/30in	White-flowered variety of common sage	Well-drained soil in sun	6-9	Seed or soft cuttings	
S.o. 'Berggarten'	h75cm/30in s75cm/30in	Larger rounded leaves coloured eau-de-nil with a tinge of grey	Well-drained soil in sun	6-9		
S.o. 'Icterina' **Golden sage**	h60cm/24in s60cm/24in	Gold-variegated leaves	Well-drained soil in sun	7-9	Seed or soft cuttings	
S.o. Purpurascens Group **Purple sage, red sage**	h75cm/30in s75cm/30in	Purple-leaved with pale blue flowers	Well-drained soil in sun	7-9	Seed or soft cuttings	
S.o. 'Purpurascens Variegata'	h75cm/30in s75cm/30in	Purple leaves splashed pink and white	Well-drained soil in sun	7-9	Seed or soft cuttings	
S.o. 'Tricolor' **Painted sage**	h45cm/18in s45cm/18in	Green leaves with white margins, flushed purple	Well-drained soil in sun	8-9	Seed or soft cuttings	
S. elegans 'Scarlet Pineapple' **Pineapple sage**	h1m/3ft s60cm/24in	Half-hardy shrubby perennial with red flowers	Well-drained soil in sun	8-9	Soft cuttings	Scented as its name implies, so use where foliage is likely to be disturbed to release scent
S. lavandulifolia **Spanish sage**	h30cm/12in s60cm/24in	Narrow-leaved and smaller-growing than common sage	Well-drained soil in sun	8-9	Soft cuttings	Can be grown and used like common sage
S. sclarea var. *turkestanica* **Biennial clary, Turkey sage**	h1.2m/4ft s1m/3ft	Biennial with broad bristly leaves and a towering flower spike of pale mauve and white bracts making it a most stately plant	Well-drained soil in sun	5-8	Seed	Self-sows readily. Uncompromising scent of foxes – or tomcat!
Sambucus nigra **Elder** Caprifoliaceae	h5m/16ft s4m/13ft	Hardy shrub or small tree with soft green leaves and whippy stems bearing saucer-sized, sweetly fragrant flower-heads, followed by clusters of shiny black berries	Well-drained or moist soil in sun or part-shade	4-8	Seed or semi-ripe cuttings	Cultivars for collection include purple-leaved 'Guincho Purple', white-variegated 'Marginata', cut-leaved f. *laciniata* and yellow 'Aurea'
Sanguisorba minor **Salad burnet** Rosaceae	h45cm/18in s30cm/12in	Soft green pinnate leaves and reddish-tinged stems; small bobble flowers best removed to preserve leaf condition	Dry soil in sun	4-7	Division or self-sown seedlings	Pretty foliage makes useful contribution to the garden and to salads
Santolina chamaecyparissus **Cotton lavender, Incana santolina** Compositae	h50cm/20in s50cm/20in	Hardy aromatic shrub with narrow, finely cut silver-grey leaves and small button-like yellow flowers in late summer	Well-drained soil in sun	6-9	Soft or semi-ripe cuttings	Clipping back hard in early spring helps to keep a tight rounded shape; can be left to flower and pruned afterwards. *S. pinnata neapolitana* 'Edward Bowles' is similar in size and habit, but the leaves

BOTANICAL NAME COMMON NAME FAMILY	HEIGHT/ SPREAD	FORM AND HABIT/ FRUIT, FOLIAGE AND FLOWERS	SITE/ SOIL	ZONES	PROPA-GATION	REMARKS
						are finer and the flowers a soft lemon-yellow
S. rosmarinifolia subsp. *rosmarinifolia*	h30cm/12in s25cm/10in	Similar to *S. chamaecyparissus* but with dark green stems	Well-drained soil in sun	6-9	Soft or semi-ripe cuttings	
Saponaria officinalis 'Rosea Plena' **Bouncing Bet, soapwort** Caryophyllaceae	h1m/3ft s1.2m/4ft	Invasive hardy perennial with soft green leaves and double pink flowers	Well-drained soil in sun	4-7	Division	The attractive flowers are tempting but remember, it needs a stern hand or it will take over the garden; perfect for diguising the garden waste dump
Satureja hortensis **Summer savory** Labiatae	h30cm/12in s15cm/6in	Twiggy little annual with highly aromatic narrow green leaves	Dry soil in sun		Seed	
S. montana **Winter savory**	h45cm/18in s45cm/18in	Evergreen shrub with narrow dark green leaves	Dry soil in sun	6-9	Division, cuttings or layering	Can be used as a low edging in formal herb gardens
Sempervivum tectorum **Houseleek** Crassulaceae	h8cm/3in s10cm/4in	Succulent perennial with tight rosettes of spiky leaves tinged red along the edges, spreads slowly to form dense hummocks covered with confetti-pink flowers in summer	Dry soil in sun	4-9	Division of offsets	Commonly seen growing on thatched cottage roofs or anchored to pantile. Also known as hen-and-chickens
Silybum marianum **Milk thistle** Compositae	h1.5m/5ft s1m/3ft	Hardy biennial. First year: broad rosette of huge prickly leaves strikingly marbled white on green; next season: tall multi-stemmed stalk bearing pink-mauve flowers	Any soil in sun or part-shade	6-9	Seed	Self-sows like a fiend, so deadhead or weed out unwanted seedlings assiduously
Smyrnium olusatrum **Alexanders, black lovage** Umbelliferae	h1.2m/4ft s1m/3ft	Upright perennial with bold glossy green foliage	Moist soil in sun or part-shade	5-9	Seed	Common in hedgerows near the sea; evergreen in mildest areas
S. perfoliatum **Alexanders**	h1m/3ft s30cm/12in	Biennial species with bright yellowy-green flowers	Moist soil in sun or part-shade	7-9	Seed	Good with spring bulbs
Solidago canadensis **Goldenrod** Compositae	h1.8m/6ft s1m/3ft	Upright-growing herbaceous perennial with lanceolate leaves and plumes of yellow sneeze-producing flowers in late summer	Well-drained or moist soil in sun or part-shade	4-8	Division	To some a pernicious weed, to others a plant of beauty. *S.* 'Crown of Rays' and 'Golden Dwarf' are perhaps more garden-worthy cultivars
Stachys officinalis **Betony, bishopswort** Labiatae	h25cm/10in s60cm/24in	Herbaceous perennial spreading by rhizomatous roots. Oval leaves are deeply toothed and the pink flower spikes appear in late summer	Moist soil in shade	5-8	Division	*S. macrantha* is similar but with corrugated dark green downy leaves and rich mauve flowers
Symphytum officinale **Comfrey** Boraginaceae	h1m/3ft s1m/3ft	Herbaceous perennial with large oval bristly leaves and nodding spikes of blue, white and purple flowers	Any soil in sun or part-shade	4-8	Seed or division	A tenacious plant; make sure you put it where you mean it to stay *S. causicum* has deep blue flowers
S. × uplandicum 'Variegatum'	h1.2m/4ft s1.2m/4ft	Like *S. officinale* and just as invasive, but with cream-variegated leaves	Any soil in sun or part-shade	4-8	Division or basal cuttings	
Tagetes patula **French marigold** Compositae	h30cm/12in s30cm/12in	Easy-to-grow annual with variably orange flowers all summer and aromatic foliage	Any soil in sun		Seed	
Tanacetum balsamita **Alecost, costmary** Compositae	h75cm/30in s30cm/12in	Herbaceous perennial with invasive creeping roots, aromatic foliage and small yellow button flowers	Well-drained soil in part-shade	5-9	Division	Cut back hard to ground level after flowering to ensure a second show of the downy grey-green foliage

BOTANICAL NAME COMMON NAME FAMILY	HEIGHT/ SPREAD	FORM AND HABIT/ FRUIT, FOLIAGE AND FLOWERS	SITE/ SOIL	ZONES	PROPA- GATION	REMARKS
T. b. var. *tanacetoides* **Camphor plant**	h1m/3ft s60cm/24in	Upright perennial with silver-grey, camphor-scented foliage and many small daisy flowers in summer	Any soil in sun	5-9	Division	
T. cinerariifolium **Pyrethrum, dalmatian pellitory** Compositae	h1.2m/4ft s1m/3ft	Herbaceous perennial with lacy grey-green leaves and white daisy flowers	Any soil in sun or part-shade	6-8	Seed or layered cuttings	
T. parthenium **Feverfew**	h30cm/12in s15cm/6in	Short-lived upright-growing perennial with soft feathery green leaves and clusters of white daisy discs	Well-drained soil in sun or part-shade	6-8	Seed	Seeds itself prolifically so you will never be without it. Will also tolerate dry soil
T. p. 'Aureum' **Golden feverfew**	h30cm/12in s15cm/6in	Particularly acid-green foliage	Well-drained soil in sun or part-shade	6-8	Seed	Seeds itself prolifically. Will also tolerate dry soil. *T. p.* 'Plenum' has daisy flowers
T. vulgare **Tansy**	h1m/3ft s45cm/18in	Herbaceous perennial that can be invasive, but worth it for the rich green ferny foliage, upright habit and clusters of yellow brass-button flowers	Well-drained moist soil in sun	4-8	Seed or division	'Silver Lace' is a pretty white-variegated cultivar
Taraxacum officinale **Dandelion** Compositae	h20cm/8in s20cm/8in	Familiar garden weed that is also a very nutritious food with a long medicinal history	Any soil in sun or shade	4-9	Seed	
Teucrium × lucidrys **Wall germander** Labiatae	h15cm/6in s30cm/12in	Evergreen shrub with tiny glossy dark green leaves and spikes of lavender-pink flowers	Well-drained soil in sun or part-shade	5-8	Division	Often wrongly listed as *T. chamaedrys*. Good for formal clipped edging
Thymus vulgaris **Common thyme, French thyme** Labiatae	h30cm/12in s30cm/12in	Bushy shrub with many tiny leaves on wiry branches and pinky-mauve flowers in summer	Dry soil in sun	4-8	Division, seed or cuttings	Common thyme makes a good low edging for formal herb gardens
T. × citriodorus **Lemon thyme**	h15cm/6in s30cm/12in	Similar to common thyme but leaves are slightly larger and shinier	Dry soil in sun	4-8	Cuttings	There are variegated and golden forms available
T. herba-barona **Caraway thyme**	h5cm/2in s30cm/12in	Dwarf shrub with caraway-scented leaves	Dry soil in sun	5-9		
T. pseudolanuginosus **Woolly thyme**	h5cm/2in s 60cm/24in	Creeping thyme that makes a mat of woolly grey leaves	Dry soil in sun	4-8	Seed or cuttings	
T. serpyllum and cultivars **Creeping thyme**	h2.5-5cm/ 1-2in s20-30cm/ 10-12in	Groundcovering dwarf shrub that makes a mat of bright colour (pink, mauve, white) when in flower	Open soil in sun	4-8	Division	
Trillium grandiflorum **Trillium, squawroot** Liliaceae/Trilliaceae	h40cm/15in s25cm/10in	Herbaceous rhizomatous perennial. The large white three-petalled flowers are held atop a narrow stem and surrounded by three heart-shaped leaves	Moist soil in shade	4-8	Division	A woodland plant
T. erectum **Beth root**	h40cm/15in s25cm/10in	As above but with purple flowers	Moist soil in shade	4-8	Division	A woodland plant

BOTANICAL NAME **COMMON NAME** FAMILY	HEIGHT/ SPREAD	FORM AND HABIT/ FRUIT, FOLIAGE AND FLOWERS	SITE/ SOIL	ZONES	PROPA- GATION	REMARKS
Tropaeolum majus **Nasturtium** Tropaeolaceae	h30cm/12in s30cm/12in	Tender annual with vivid scarlet, orange and yellow flowers	Well-drained soil in sun or part-shade		Seed	
T. majus 'Empress of India'	h1.5m/5ft s1m/3ft	Tender annual with vermilion flowers	Well-drained soil in sun or part-shade		Seed	Vigorous climbing relative of *T. m.* with rich red flowers and dark blue-green leaves
Valeriana officinalis **Valerian, all heal, garden heliotrope** Valerianaceae	h1.2m/4ft s1m/3ft	Rhizomatous perennial with attractive heart-shaped foliage and umbels of white to pinky-mauve flowers	Well-drained moist soil in part-shade or sun	5-9	Division	*V. phu* 'Aurea' has good yellow foliage in spring
Veratrum species **False hellebores** Liliaceae/Melanthiaceae	h1.2m/4ft s45cm/18in	Herbaceous perennials valuable for the hosta-like foliage that is deeply pleated	Well-drained soil in part-shade	5-8	Seed or division	A showcase plant, with leaves like soft green Fortuny fabric, for a shady corner
Verbascum thapsus **Mullein, Aaron's rod** Scrophulariaceae	h1.8m/6ft s1m/3ft	Biennial making a broad rosette of heavily felted leaves from which rises a towering fuzzy stalk covered with soft yellow flowers	Well-drained soil in sun	3-8	Seed	It will seed itself anywhere so watch that it does not smother a weaker border companion
V. lychnitis **White mullein**	h75cm-1.2m/ 30in-4ft s45cm/18in	Native biennial with dark green leaves, powdery white underneath, and branched spikes of white or yellow flowers	Well-drained soil in sun	5-9	Seed	
V. nigrum **Black mullein**	h60cm-1m/ 24in-3ft s45cm/18in	Similar to white mullein but with darker leaves. Flowers usually yellow, though occasionally white	As above	5-9	Seed	
Verbena bonariensis Verbenaceae	h1.5m/5ft s60cm/24in	Perennial with reed-like wiry stems and coarse dark green leaves topped in late summer by clusters of tiny lilac flowers with orange throats	Any soil in sun or part-shade	7-9	Seed	
V. officinalis **Vervain**	h60cm/24in s15cm/6in	Hardy perennial with soft green, lobed leaves and tiny pale lavender flowers along the wiry flower stems	As above	4-9	Seed or division	Said to 'rob witches of their will'. *V. × hybrida* is the tender perennial used in bedding schemes, 'Silver Anne' and 'Sissinghurst' being especially popular
Vinca major **Greater periwinkle** Apocynaceae	h15cm/6in s indefinite	Creeping evergreen groundcover with tubular bright blue or white flowers	Any soil in sun or part-shade	4-8	Rooted runners	
V. minor **Lesser periwinkle**	h60cm/24in s indefinite	Perennial groundcovering shrub. Flower stalks bearing bright blue flowers in the axils of the shiny green leaves arise along the length of the stems	Any soil in sun or part-shade	4-8	Rooted runners	The long trailing stems root as they travel. *Vinca minor* 'Argenteovariegata' is a Saxon herb known as 'joy of the ground'
Viola odorata **Sweet violet** Violaceae	h25cm/10in s15cm/6in	Herbaceous perennial forming clumps of heart-shaped leaves with sweetly scented purple flowers	Well-drained moist soil in sun	4-8	Division	There are many named cultivars with varying flowers, colours and scent strength
V. tricolor **Heartsease, Johnny jump-up**	h15cm/6in s10cm/4in	Small cheery-faced pansy	Well-drained moist soil in sun	3-8	Self-sown seed	

USEFULNESS ZONES

The Usefulness Zones given for each plant represent the range of zones in which the plant may be successfully grown. The lower figure gives the coldest zone in which the plant will be hardy without winter protection; the higher shows the limit of its tolerance of hot summer weather. The chart on the right gives the average annual minimum temperature of each zone.

The zone ratings given here are based on those devised by the United States Department of Agriculture and zones are allocated to plants according to their tolerance of conditions typical of North America. These zones also apply, broadly, in Australia and in continental Europe. In the British Isles and most of New Zealand, where hot, dry summers are rare, the upper zone does not usually present a limitation. Generally, gardeners in Britain and New Zealand need only take into consideration the lower zone.

It must be remembered that zoning data can only be a rough guide. Plant hardiness depends on a great many factors, and within any one zone particular regions may be endowed with more or less favourable conditions, just as on a smaller scale in any one garden plants can be positioned in individual situations that will suit their needs to a greater or lesser extent.

CELSIUS	ZONES	°FAHRENHEIT
Below -45	1	Below -50
-45 to -40	2	-50 to - 40
-40 to -34	3	-40 to -30
-34 to -29	4	-30 to -20
-29 to -23	5	-20 to -10
-23 to -18	6	-10 to 0
-18 to -12	7	0 to 10
-12 to -7	8	10 to 20
-7 to -1	9	20 to 30
-1 to 4	10	30 to 40
above 4	11	above 40

Useful Addresses

The following addresses include nurseries dedicated to herbs, and others where you can obtain herbs and related plants.

UK

Barwinnock Herbs, Barrhill, Ayrshire KA26 ORB

Bernwode Plants, The Thatched Cottage, Duck Lane, Ludgershall, Aylesbury, Buckinghamshire HP18 9NZ

Caroline Holmes Herbs, Denham End Farm, Denham, Bury St Edmunds, Suffolk IP29 5EE

Cheshire Herbs, Fourfields, Forest Road, Little Budworth, nr Tarporley, Cheshire CW6 9ES

Chiltern Seeds, Bortree Stile, Ulverston, Cumbria LA12 7PB (Everything you could possibly want to grow from seed!)

Daphne Ffiske Herbs, Rosemary Cottage, Bramerton, Norwich, Norfolk NR14 7DW

Herterton House, Hartingdon, Cambo, Morpeth, Northumberland (Physic garden and nursery with unusual plants)

Hexham Herbs, The Chesters Walled Garden, Holders of the National Thyme Collection

Hoecroft Plants, Severals Grange, Wood Norton, Dereham, Norfolk NR20 5BL

Hollington Nurseries, Berkshire RG15 9XT

Jekka's Herb Farm, Rose Cottage, Shellards Lane, Alveston, Bristol, Avon BA12 2SY

Lower Severalls Herb Nursery, Crewkerne, Somerset TA18 7NX

Monksilver Nursery, Oakington Road, Cottenham, Cambridgeshire CB4 4TW

Norfolk Herbs, Blackberry Farm, Dereham Road, Dillington, Dereham, Norfolk NR19 2QD

Norfolk Lavender, Caley Mill, Heacham, King's Lynn, Norfolk PE31 7JE

Raveningham Gardens, Norwich, Norfolk NR14 6NS (Plants for foliage, bark & berries)

Read's Nursery, Hales Hall, Loddon, Norfolk NR14 6QW (Conservatory plants, vines, citrus, figs and unusual fruit, scented and aromatic plants)

Suffolk Herbs, Monks Farm, Pantlings Lane, Kelvedon, Essex CO5 9PG

USA

Alyce's Herbs, PO Box 9563, Madison, WI 53715

Bo's Nursery, 12743 Gillard Road, Winter Garden, FL 01969

Cricket Hill Herb Farm Ltd, Glen Street, Rowley, MA 01969

Dutch Mill Herb Farm, Route 2, Box 190, Forest Grove, OR 97116

The Gathered Herb and Greenhouse, 12114 N. State Road, Otisville, MI 48463

Glade Valley Nursery, 9226 Links Road, Walkersville, MD 21793

The Gourmet Gardener, 4000 W 126th Street, Leawood, KS 66209

Heronwood Nursery, 7530 288th Street, NE, Kingston, WA 98346 (Less common plants including Asiatic species)

Kurt Bluemel Inc., 2740 Greene Lane, Baldwin, MD 21013 (Ornamental grasses, hedges, bamboos, etc.; also aquatics)

Plants of the Southwest, 930 Baca Street, Santa Fe, NM 87501(Seed and plants native to south-western states)

Rasland Farm, NC82 at US 13, Godwin, NC 28344-9712

Sandy Mush Herb Nursery, Route 2, Surret Cove Rd, Leicester, NC 28748

Stallings Nursery, 910 Encinitas Blvd, Encinitas, CA 92024 (Many subtropical plants, including bamboo and bananas)

Sunnybrook Farms Nursery, 9448 Mayfield Road, PO Box 6, Chesterland, OH 44026 (Herbs; also hostas, ivies and scented pelargoniums)

Taylor's Herb Gardens, 1535 Lone Oak Road, Vista, CA 92084

Well-sheep Herb Farm, 317 Mt Bethel Road, Port Murray, NJ 07865

Yucca Do at Peckerwood Gardens, PM 359, PO Box 655, Waller, TX 77484 (Plants from the south-west, including Texas and northern Mexico)

AUSTRALIA

Bridestowe Lavender Farm, Nabowla, TAS 7254

Bush Garden, Salamanca Market, Hobart, TAS (By appointment: phone 002 233 481)

Chandler's Nursery, 75 Queen Street, Sandy Bay, TAS 7005

Digger's Seeds, 105 Latrobe Parade, Dramana, VIC 3936

Herbage Herb Garden and Nursery, 3 Gent Street, Ballarat, VIC 3356

Hillside Herbs, RSD Truscott Road, McLaren Flat, SA 5171

Kings Herb Seeds, PO Box 14, Glenbrook, NSW 2773

Lillydale Herb Farm, 61 Mangans Road, Lilydale, VIC 3140

L. O'Dea Herbs, 5 Ellelong Street, Kearsley, NSW 2325

Meadow Herbs, Simms Road, Mt Baker (PO Box 57), SA 5251

Norfolk Punch Gardens, Batar Creek Road, Kendall, NSW 2439

Pennyroyal Herbs, Penny's Lane, Branym, Bundaberg, QLD 4670

The Perfumed Garden 559 Portrush Road, Glenunga, SA 5064

Phoenix Seeds, PO Box 9, Stanley, TAS 7331

Redcliffe Education Centre, Henzell Street, Redcliffe, QLD 4020

Thurlby Herb Farm, Gardiner Road, Walpole, WA 6398

Villarett Gardens and Tea House, RSD 237, Moltema, TAS 7304

Vuolong Lavender Estate, Vendon Road, Mt Egerton, VIC 3345

Woodbank Nursery, Huon Highway, Longley, TAS 7103

NEW ZEALAND
Karamea Herbs, Tuhikaramea Road, RD 2 Pukekohe, Auckland

Somerfields, PO Box 10133, Phillipstown, Christchurch

DENMARK
Annemette Oleson, Skarresøhus, Ballevej 27, Skavvesø, 8550 Ryomagård

Købstadsmuseet, 8000 Århus C, DK

Vitskøl Kloster, Viborgvej 475, 9681 Ranum

FRANCE
Fragrance, 71110 Varenne-l'Aroconce

Un Jardin de Cottage, Monique Hego, 4 rue Laurent Pillard, 8810 Saint-Die-des-Vosges

Martine Lemonier, Établissements Horticoles du Coudray, 76850 Bose-le-Hard, Normandie

Monique Fehr-Forestie, Maleychard du Haut Castex, 09350 Daumazan, Arize

GERMANY
'Duft-un Tastgarten' Deutschen Medizinhistorischen Museum, Ingoldstadt, Germany. (A physic garden for taste and smell, based on the original *hortus medico-botanicus* at the University of Ingoldstadt, which was Europe's oldest medical school; the building now houses a museum of medical history.)

NORWAY
Grethe Gerhardsen Treland, Urtehagen i Bjorkeliveien 2, Kjos Haveby, N-4622, Kritiansand (Plants, classes in herbal preparations, culinary uses and herb gardening)

Hildurs Urterarium, 8900 Brønnøgsund

SWEDEN
Ortagården i Mulltorp, V/ Mary Johannson, Mulltorp 2051, 44092 Svanesund

Tirups ortagård, V/ Eva Falck, 24500 Staffenstorp

The following are just a few of the many display gardens devoted to herbs or featuring herbs as part of a historic display. All are worth visiting.

UK
The American Museum, Claverton Manor, Bath

Chelsea Physic Garden, Royal Hospital Road, London SW1

Harlow Car Gardens, Harrogate

Museum of Garden History, St Mary-at-Lambeth, London SE1

Royal Botanic Gardens, Kew, Surrey

The Tudor Garden Museum, St Michael's Square, Southampton

USA
Brooklyn Botanic Garden, 1000 Washington Avenue, Brooklyn, New York, NY 11225

Huntingdon Library & Botanical Gardens, 1151 Oxford Road, San Marino, CA 91108

Longwood Gardens, Kennet Square, PA 19348

The National Herb Garden at the National Arboretum, 3501 New York Avenue, NE Washington, DC 20002

The New York Botanical Garden, 200th Street & Southern Blvd, Bronx, NY 10458

University of California Botanical Gardens, Centennial Drive, Berkeley, CA 94720

Western Reserve Herb Garden at Greater Cleveland Garden Centre, University Circle, Cleveland, OH 44106

AUSTRALIA
'Birchfield', 31 Turallo Terrace, Bungendore, NSW 2621 (Check annual garden open listings for opening dates and times.)

Mt Tomah Botanic Gardens, Bells Line of Road, via Bilpin, NSW 2758

Royal Botanical Gardens, The Domain, Hobart, TAS 7000

Royal Botanical Gardens, Mt Coot-tha, QLD 4066

Royal Botanical Gardens, Mrs Macquarie's Road, Sydney, NSW 2000

Royal Botanic Gardens, Birdwood Avenue, South Yarra, VIC 3141

GROUPS AND SOCIETIES
The Herb Society, 134 Buckingham Palace Road, London SW1 9AS, UK

The Herb Society of America, 9019 Kirtland Chardon Road, Mentor, OH 44060, USA

The Australian Herb Society, PO Box 110, Mapleton, QLD 4560, Australia

The Australian Garden History Society, Royal Botanic Gardens, Birdwood Avenue, South Yarra, VIC 3141, Australia

Herb Federation of New Zealand, PO Box 007, Christchurch, New Zealand

Further Reading

Brooklyn Botanic Garden. *Oriental Herbs and Vegetables,* New York, 1983

Chatto, Beth. *The Dry Garden,* J. M. Dent & Sons, London, 1978

Clarke, Ethne. *The Art of the Kitchen Garden,* Michael Joseph, London, 1988

Cuffley, Peter. *Cottage Gardens in Australia,* Five Mile Press, Victoria, 1983

Glattstein, Judy. *Garden Design with Foliage,* Garden Way, Vermont, 1991

Grieve, Mrs M. *A Modern Herbal,* Jonathan Cape 1931 (Revised edition: Penguin Books, London, 1980)

Grigson, Geoffrey. *The Englishman's Flora,* Phoenix House, London, 1955

Hansen, Richard & Frederick Stahl. *Perennials and their Garden Habitats,* Cambridge University Press, Cambridge, 1993

Hayward, Gordon. *Garden Paths,* Camden House Publishing, Vermont, 1993

Miller, Amy. *Shaker Herbs,* Clarkson N. Potter, New York, 1976

Nottle, Trevor. *Old-fashioned Gardens,* Kangaroo Press, Kenthurst, New South Wales, Australia, 1992

Paterson, Allen. *Herbs in the Garden,* J. M. Dent, London, 1985

Paterson, Allen. 'Origins of the Ornamental Herb Garden', *Hortus,* Vol. III, Farnham, Surrey, 1987

Philips, Roger, & Nicky Foy. *Herbs,* Pan Books, London, 1990

Pleasant, Barbara. *Warm Climate Gardening,* Garden Way, Vermont, 1993

Reid, Daniel P. *Chinese Herbal Medicine,* Shambhala, Boston, 1993

Sanecki, Kay N. *History of the English Herb Garden,* Ward Lock, London, 1992

Segall, Barbara. *The Herb Garden Month by Month,* David & Charles, Newton Abbott, Devon, 1994

Sinclair Rohde, Eleanour. *Herbs and Herb Gardening,* Medici Society, London, 1936

Verey, Rosemary. *The Scented Garden,* Michael Joseph, London, 1981

Walling, Edna. *A Gardener's Log,* Oxford University Press, Oxford, 1948 (Revised edition: Anne O'Donovan Pty, Victoria, 1992)

Wrensch, Ruth. *The Essence of Herbs,* University of Mississippi Press, Mississippi, 1992

Index

Figures in *italic* type refer to photographs and their captions and to planting plans.

Acknowledgments

Author's Acknowledgments

This is the most difficult part of any book to write: mere words hardly seem adequate to express the gratitude Clive and I feel for the kindness of all the people who have allowed us to use their gardens. I have learned so much from each person I met and invariably enjoyed our conversations about every aspect of herbs, about the pleasure and pains of garden-making and the memories of past achievements and disasters, and sharing our plans for future garden glories. Without their generosity I could not have written this book.

Specifically, they are: Wendy Francis, The Anchorage in Kent, a garden that is a distillation of all that is good about Sissinghurst; Carla Carlisle, Wyken Hall, Suffolk (whose vineyards and first-class restaurant refreshed the parts overawed by the garden); and Christine Forecast, at whose Congham Hall Country House Hotel in Norfolk, you can stay to enjoy the herb garden at first hand – pure bliss.

Brian and Rosemary Clifton-Sprigg at Norfolk Herbs, Blackberry Farm, Dillington, Dereham, Norfolk, offer an extensive collection of well-grown herb plants – and are brilliant at planting up containers. If you need to know more about thyme (who doesn't?) visit Kevin and Susie White at Hexham Herbs, Chesters Walled Garden, Humshaugh, Northumberland; they have countless other herbs as well. One garden in particular was an inspiration: Herterton House, Cambo, near Morpeth in Northumberland. In addition to the Physic Garden, Frank and Marjorie Lawley have created a most exquisite pleasure garden, as intricately patterned as an oriental carpet and glowing with the jewelled colour of a sunlit stained-glass window. Their nursery is a source of choice plants, many collected and introduced by the Lawleys;

the gardening world owes them a huge debt of gratitude. Lord and Lady Tollemache at Helmingham Hall in Suffolk have welcomed me repeatedly to their garden. It should be on every garden visit list for the splendour of its setting and the old world charm of the garden itself.

I am profoundly grateful to the garden designer Pam Lewis, of Sticky Wicket, Buckland Newton, near Dorchester, Dorset; her colour-wheel garden is simply breathtaking. My thanks also to Lucy Huntingdon and Mark Walker, who allowed me to use their Chelsea Flower Show gardens – respectively, the low-allergen garden and the Cartier and *Harpers & Queen* classical garden, constructed by Clifton Landscape and Design; and to Audrey and Mary Pring, Lower Severalls, Crewkerne, Somerset. Elizabeth Oeleris, a sculptor who gardens near Dieppe, has turned her talents to making a relaxing garden picture that will draw me back again.

Without Erica Hunningher at Frances Lincoln, I would not have had the chance to write this book, so heartfelt thanks to her and to Jo Christian, Penelope Miller, Penny David and Trish Going, who pulled it all together. Mr Creosote made sure we always ate well. Jane and Donald kept the home fires burning.

It is to my friends that I owe the greatest debt for inspiration, consolation, encouragement and education: Alan Gray and Graham Robeson at the Old Vicarage, East Ruston, in Norfolk, Marilyn Godden (another artist with considerable talent for garden-making) and the landscape designer Mark Brown, whose garden at Le Berquerie, Varengeville-sur-Mer, was my personal road to Damascus.

This book is for you, Ray Bob.

Publishers' Acknowledgments

The publishers wish to offer special thanks to Antonia Johnson for her help in producing this book.

Horticultural Consultant Tony Lord
Editors Penelope Miller and Penny David
Art Editor Patricia Going
Picture Editor Anne Fraser
Indexer Penny David
Production Adela Cory
Editorial assistance Helen Cleary

Editorial Director Erica Hunningher
Art Director Caroline Hillier
Production Director Nicky Bowden

Photographic Acknowledgments

t = top   l = left
b = below   r = right

All photographs copyright © Clive Nichols, except for the following:
Deni Bown 37, 39b, 50, 51bl and br, 72, 73, 83tl and bl, 91l, 96b

Neil Campbell-Sharp 2, 53

Geoff Dann © FLL 65, 96t

Andrew Lawson 70, © FLL 51t, 105

Roger Phillips © FLL 39t, 102r